HOW TO MAKE A MINNESOTA WILL

Second Edition

D-M Boulay
Mark Warda
Attorneys at Law

SPHINX® PUBLISHING
AN IMPRINT OF SOURCEBOOKS, INC.®
NAPERVILLE, ILLINOIS

Second Edition, 2002

Published by: **Sphinx® Publishing, An Imprint of Sourcebooks, Inc.®**

<u>Naperville Office</u>
P.O. Box 4410
Naperville, Illinois 60567-4410
630-961-3900
Fax: 630-961-2168
http://www.sphinxlegal.com
http://www.sourcebooks.com

This publication is designed to provide accurate and authoritative information in regard to the subject matter covered. It is sold with the understanding that the publisher is not engaged in rendering legal, accounting, or other professional service. If legal advice or other expert assistance is required, the services of a competent professional person should be sought.

From a Declaration of Principles Jointly Adopted by a Committee of the
American Bar Association and a Committee of Publishers and Associations

This product is not a substitute for legal advice.

Disclaimer required by Texas statutes.

Library of Congress Cataloging-in-Publication Data
Boulay, D.-M. (Donna-Marie), 1942-
  How to make a Minnesota will / D-M Boulay, Mark Warda.-- 2nd ed.
    p. cm.
  Rev. ed. of: How to make a Minnesota will / Elizabeth J. Wolf, Mark Warda. 1st ed. 1996.
  Includes index.
  ISBN 1-57248-178-1 (alk. paper)
  1. Wills--Minnesota--Popular works. I. Warda, Mark. II. Wolf, Elizabeth J. How to make a Minnesota will. III. Title.

KFM5544.Z9 W65 2002
346.77605'4--dc21   2001049900

Printed and bound in the United States of America.

VHG Paperback — 10 9 8 7 6 5 4 3 2 1

CONTENTS

USING SELF-HELP
LAW BOOKS

Before using a self-help law book, you should realize the advantages and disadvantages of doing your own legal work and understand the challenges and diligence that this requires.

THE GROWING
TREND

Rest assured that you won't be the first or only person handling your own legal matter. For example, in some states, more than seventy-five percent of divorces and other cases have at least one party representing him or herself. Because of the high cost of legal services, this is a major trend and many courts are struggling to make it easier for people to represent themselves. However, some courts are not happy with people who do not use attorneys and refuse to help them in any way. For some, the attitude is, "Go to the law library and figure it out for yourself."

We at Sphinx write and publish self-help law books to give people an alternative to the often complicated and confusing legal books found in most law libraries. We have made the explanations of the law as simple and easy to understand as possible. Of course, unlike an attorney advising an individual client, we cannot cover every conceivable possibility.

COST/VALUE
ANALYSIS

Whenever you shop for a product or service, you are faced with various levels of quality and price. In deciding what product or service to buy, you make a cost/value analysis on the basis of your willingness to pay and the quality you desire.

When buying a car, you decide whether you want transportation, comfort, status, or sex appeal. Accordingly, you decide among such choices as a Neon, a Lincoln, a Rolls Royce, or a Porsche. Before making a decision, you usually weigh the merits of each option against the cost.

When you get a headache, you can take a pain reliever (such as aspirin) or visit a medical specialist for a neurological examination. Given this choice, most people, of course, take a pain reliever, since it costs only pennies; whereas a medical examination costs hundreds of dollars and takes a lot of time. This is usually a logical choice because it is rare to need anything more than a pain reliever for a headache. But in some cases, a headache may indicate a brain tumor and failing to see a specialist right away can result in complications. Should everyone with a headache go to a specialist? Of course not, but people treating their own illnesses must realize that they are betting on the basis of their cost/value analysis of the situation. They are taking the most logical option.

The same cost/value analysis must be made when deciding to do one's own legal work. Many legal situations are very straight forward, requiring a simple form and no complicated analysis. Anyone with a little intelligence and a book of instructions can handle the matter without outside help.

But there is always the chance that complications are involved that only an attorney would notice. To simplify the law into a book like this, several legal cases often must be condensed into a single sentence or paragraph. Otherwise, the book would be several hundred pages long and too complicated for most people. However, this simplification necessarily leaves out many details and nuances that would apply to special or unusual situations. Also, there are many ways to interpret most legal questions. Your case may come before a judge who disagrees with the analysis of our authors.

Therefore, in deciding to use a self-help law book and to do your own legal work, you must realize that you are making a cost/value analysis. You have decided that the money you will save in doing it yourself outweighs the chance that your case will not turn out to your satisfaction. Most people handling their own simple legal matters never have a problem, but occasionally people find that it ended up costing them more to have an attorney straighten out the situation than it would have if they had hired an attorney in the beginning. Keep this in mind if you decide to handle your own case, and be sure to consult an attorney if you feel you might need further guidance.

LOCAL RULES   The next thing to remember is that a book which covers the law for the entire nation, or even for an entire state, cannot possibly include every procedural difference of every county court. Whenever possible, we provide the exact form needed; however, in some areas, each county, or even each judge, may require unique forms and procedures. In our *state* books, our forms usually cover the majority of counties in the state, or provide examples of the type of form that will be required. In our *national* books, our forms are sometimes even more general in nature but are designed to give a good idea of the type of form that will be needed in most locations. Nonetheless, keep in mind that your *state*, county, or judge may have a requirement, or use a form, that is not included in this book.

You should not necessarily expect to be able to get all of the information and resources you need solely from within the pages of this book. This book will serve as your guide, giving you specific information whenever possible and helping you to find out what else you will need to know. This is just like if you decided to build your own backyard deck. You might purchase a book on how to build decks. However, such a book would not include the building codes and permit requirements of every city, town, county, and township in the nation; nor would it include the lumber, nails, saws, hammers, and other materials and tools you would need to actually build the deck. You would use the book as your guide, and then do some work and research involving such matters as whether you need a permit of some kind, what type and grade of wood are available in your area, whether to use hand tools or power tools, and how to use those tools.

Before using the forms in a book like this, you should check with your court clerk to see if there are any local rules of which you should be aware, or local forms you will need to use. Often, such forms will require the same information as the forms in the book but are merely laid out differently, use slightly different language, or use different color paper so the clerks can easily find them. They will sometimes require additional information.

CHANGES IN THE LAW

Besides being subject to state and local rules and practices, the law is subject to change at any time. The courts and the legislatures of all fifty states are constantly revising the laws. It is possible that while you are reading this book, some aspect of the law is being changed or that a court is interpreting a law in a different way. You should always check the most recent statutes, rules and regulations to see what, if any changes have been made.

In most cases, the change will be of minimal significance. A form will be redesigned, additional information will be required, or a waiting period will be extended. As a result, you might need to revise a form, file an extra form, or wait out a longer time period; these types of changes will not usually affect the outcome of your case. On the other hand, sometimes a major part of the law is changed, the entire law in a particular area is rewritten, or a case that was the basis of a central legal point is overruled. In such instances, your entire ability to pursue your case may be impaired.

Again, you should weigh the value of your case against the cost of an attorney and make a decision as to what you believe is in your best interest.

INTRODUCTION

This book was written to help Minnesota residents quickly and easily make their own wills without the expense or delay of hiring a lawyer. It begins with a short explanation of how a will works and what a will can and cannot do. It is designed to allow those with simple estates to quickly and inexpensively set up their affairs to distribute their property according to their wishes. It includes an explanation of how such things as joint property and *pay on death* accounts will affect your planning.

It also includes information on appointing a guardian for any minor children you may have. This can be useful in avoiding bad feelings between relatives and in protecting the children from being raised by someone you would object to.

Chapters 1 through 5 and Chapter 7 explain the laws that affect the making of a will. Chapter 6 describes advance health care directives. There is a glossary of terms after the chapters. Appendix A contains Internet sites to assist you with the details of your planning. Appendix B has sample filled-in will forms to show you how it is done. Appendix C contains blank will forms you can use. A flow chart in Appendix C, page 72 will help you choose the right will form based upon your circumstances and desires.

You can prepare your own will quickly and easily by using the forms out of the book by photocopying them, or you can retype the material on sheets of paper. The small amount of time it takes to do this can give you and your loved ones the peace of mind of knowing that your estate will be distributed according to your wishes.

However, persons who draft their own wills should do so with great caution. Just because the forms are so easily available does not mean that they apply to your situation. Although the basic forms in this book are excellent, none of them are substitutes for experienced legal or financial advice when you need help tailored to your particular needs and wants.

Self-drawn up wills can be especially vulnerable in Minnesota because the form of the will is tightly regulated by statutes and case law. If that form is not precisely followed, a court could decide that a will is no good. That could cause your loved ones tragic and costly problems.

Remember that by the time your will is supposed to go into effect, you are not around to work on getting the problems solved. If a court holds your will invalid all your work to make your will, with all of your good intentions, could easily be for nothing.

Keep all of these alerts in mind as you approach one of life's most serious and important decisions, the transfer of your money and your property the way you want. Be sure to consult an attorney or financial or other professional at any point if you feel you might need further guidance.

If you do decide to consult with an attorney or financial professional, you don't have to turn over the whole project to them. But try to find those who are experienced and knowledgeable in the specific areas in which you need help.

A surprising number of people have had their estates pass to the wrong parties because of a simple lack of knowledge of how the laws work. Before using any of the forms in Appendix C, you should read and understand all of the previous chapters of this book.

In each example given in the text you might ask, "What if the spouse died first?" or "What if the children were grown up?" and then the answer might be different. Remember, if your situation is at all complicated, you are advised to seek the advice of an attorney. No book of this type can cover every contingency in every case, but a knowledge of the basics will help you to make the right decisions regarding your property.

NOTE: *The forms in this book are for simple wills to leave property to your family, or if you have no family, to friends or charities. As explained in Chapter 2, if you wish to disinherit your family and leave your property to others, you should consult with an attorney who can be sure that your will cannot be successfully challenged in court.*

KNOWING THE BASIC RULES

1

Before making your will, you should understand how a will works and what it can and cannot do. Otherwise, your plans may not be carried out and the wrong people may end up with your property.

WILL DEFINED

A *will* is a gift of property that takes effect only at death. It is the document you use to control who gets your property, who will be guardian of your children and their property, and who will manage your estate upon your death. It is the solemn disposition of your property.

HOW A WILL IS USED

Some people think a will avoids *probate*—the legal process used to establish the legal validity of a will. It does not. A will is the document used in probate to determine who receives the property, and who is appointed guardian and executor or *personal representative*.

AVOIDING PROBATE

If you wish to avoid probate you need to use methods other than a will, such as *joint ownership, pay-on-death accounts,* or *living trusts*. The first two of these are discussed later in this chapter. For information on living trusts you should refer to a book that focuses on trusts as used for estate planning.

If a person successfully avoids probate with all of his or her property, then he or she may not need a will. In most cases, when a husband or wife dies, no will or probate is necessary because everything is owned jointly. However, everyone should have a will in case some property, that one forgot to put into joint ownership or that was received just prior to death, does not avoid probate for some reason, or if both husband and wife die in the same accident.

JOINT TENANCY AND PROBATE

Property that is owned in *joint tenancy with right of survivorship* does not pass under a will. If a will gives property to one person but it is already in a joint account with another person, the will is usually ignored and the joint owner of the account gets the property. This is because the property in the account avoids probate and passes directly to the joint owner. A will only controls property that goes through probate. There are exceptions to this rule. If money is put into a joint account only for convenience, it might pass under the will; but if the joint owner does not give it up, it could take an expensive court battle to get it back.

Putting property into joint tenancy does not give absolute rights to it. If the estate owes estate taxes, the recipient of joint tenancy property may have to contribute to the tax payment. Also, some states give spouses a right to property that is in joint accounts with other people. This is explained later in this chapter on page 4.

Example 1: Ted and his wife want all of their property to go to the survivor of them. They put their house, cars, bank accounts, and brokerage accounts in joint ownership. When Ted dies his wife only has to show his death certificate to get all the property transferred to her name. No probate or will is necessary.

Example 2: After Ted's death, his wife, Michelle puts all of the property and accounts into joint ownership with her son, Mark. Upon Michelle's death, Mark needs only to present her death certificate to have everything transferred into his name. No probate or will is necessary.

JOINT TENANCY AND YOUR WILL

If all property is in joint ownership or if all property is distributed through a will, things are simple. But when some property passes by each method, a person's plans may not be fulfilled.

Example 1: Bill's will leaves all his property to his sister, Mary. Bill dies owning a house jointly with his wife, Joan, and a bank account jointly with his son, Don. Upon Bill's death Joan gets the house, Don gets the bank account and his sister, Mary, gets nothing.

Example 2: Betty's will leaves half her assets to Ann and half her assets to George. Betty dies owning $1,000,000 in stock jointly with George, and a car in her name alone. Ann gets to own only half of the car, George gets to own the other half of the car and all of the stock.

Example 3: John's will leaves all his property equally to his five children. Before going in the hospital he puts his oldest son, Harry, as a joint owner of his accounts. John dies and Harry gets all of his assets. The rest of the children get nothing.

In each of these cases the property went to a person it probably should not have because the decedent did not realize that joint ownership overruled his or her will. In some families this might not be a problem. Harry might divide the property equally (and possibly pay a gift tax). But in many cases Harry would just keep everything and the family would never talk to him again, or would take him to court.

JOINT TENANCY AND RISKS

In many cases joint property can be an ideal way to own property and avoid probate. However it does have risks. If you put your real estate in joint ownership with someone, you cannot sell it or mortgage it without that person's signature. If you put your bank account in joint ownership with someone they can take out all of your money.

Example 1: Alice put her house in joint ownership with her son. She later married Ed and moved in with him. She wanted to sell her house and to invest the money for income. Her son refused to sign the deed because he wanted to keep the home in the family. She was in court for ten months getting her house back and the judge almost refused to do it.

Example 2: Alex put his bank accounts into joint ownership with his daughter Mary to avoid probate. Mary fell in love with Doug who was in trouble with the law. Doug talked Mary into "borrowing" $30,000 from the account for a "business deal" that went sour. Later she "borrowed" $25,000 more to pay Doug's bail bond. Alex did not find out until it was too late that his money was gone.

FIVE TYPICAL WAYS TO OWN PROPERTY AND ASSETS IN MINNESOTA

Minnesota law offers you several options for how to hold title to property in Minnesota. You can choose the option that fits your situation for each one of your financial holdings and pieces of real estate. The following list contains descriptions in a nutshell of complicated legal principals to help you make your decisions. To help you evaluate which will work best for your intentions, you may want to consult with a financial or legal professional.

1. *Separate ownership.* This is when the title to your property and all of your financial assets are in your name only—owned only by you.

2. *Joint tenancy.* This is when two or more people are on the title and there is the right of survivorship. This means that upon the death of one person, the person or persons who are on the title automatically acquire the property or other assets.

Example: Tom and Marcia bought a house together and lived together for twenty years but were never married. The deed did not specify joint tenancy. When Tom died, his brother inherited his half of the house and it had to be sold because Marcia could not afford to buy it from him.

3. *Tenants in Common*. This means when one owner dies, that owner's share of the property or other assets goes to his or her heirs or beneficiaries under the will.

Example: Lindsay and her husband Rocky bought a house. When Rocky suddenly died, Lindsay obtained full ownership of the house by filing a death certificate at the courthouse. That was because the deed to the house stated that they were husband and wife so ownership was presumed to be join tenancy.

4. *Life Estate*. This is most often used by very elderly people whose home is their biggest asset.

Example: A widow gives her interest in her home to her daughter in a quit claim deed. This allows the mother to stay in the home as long as she lives. She is responsible for all the taxes, upkeep, and other financial obligations of the home. When the mother dies, the daughter automatically owns it. The chief advantage of this technique is that it avoids probate.

5. *Trust Ownership*. This is when the title to property and other assets are put into a trust. Trusts are helpful to people with a lot money, as a way to protect spendthrift heirs. They avoid probate and can be used to describe how assets are to be managed if the owner is incapacitated. Trusts are beyond the scope of this book.

YOUR SPOUSE

Under Minnesota law a surviving spouse is entitled to a percentage of a person's estate no matter what the person's will states. This is called the *elective share*. It is meant to protect a spouse from being left destitute.

The percentage, called the elective share, is listed in the Minnesota Probate Code, Section 524.2-202. The percentage depends on the number of years you have been married. For those married at least one year, it is 3%. For those married 15 years or more, it is 50%. The percent is taken from the augmented estate. *Augmented* refers to the total value of the estate. This amount excludes the value of your permanent legal residence located in Minnesota.

Number of years married to each other:	Amount of elective share
Less than one year	depends on amount of marital assets
One year but less than 2	3%
Two years but less than 3	6%
Three years but less than 4	9%
Four years but less than 5	12%
Five years but less than 6	15%
Six years but less than 7	18%
Seven years but less than 8	21%
Eight years but less than 9	24%
Nine years but less than 10	27%
Ten years but less than 11	30%
11 years but less than 12	34%
12 years but less than 13	38%
13 years but less than 14	42%
14 years but less than 15	46%
15 years or more	50%

Example 1: John's will leave all of his property to his children of a prior marriage and nothing to his second wife who is already wealthy. The wife still gets a percentage of John's estate and his children divide the rest.

Example 2: Mary puts half of her property in a joint account with her husband and in her will she leaves all of her other property to her sister. When she dies, her husband gets all the money in the joint account and a percent of all her other property.

If you do not plan to leave your spouse at least the percentage of your estate required by Minnesota Statutes, you should consult a lawyer. (Minn.Stat. Ann., Sec. 524.2-202.)

A Spouse's Share

While some feel it is wrong to avoid giving a spouse the share allowed by law, there are legitimate reasons for doing so (such as where both spouses are wealthy and there are children from a prior marriage) and the law allows exceptions.

The easiest way is for your spouse to sign a written agreement either before or after the marriage. While many spouses express the greatest fondness for their stepchildren, getting them to sign over a large share of an estate can be a challenge. When such an agreement is signed before marriage it is called a *premarital agreement* or *antenuptial agreement* and when it is signed during the marriage it is called a *spousal consent*.

To avoid a spouse's share without his or her knowledge opens the door wide for the possibility of a lawsuit after your death. If your actions were not done to the precise legal requirements of spousal consent or prenuptial agreements they could be thrown out and your spouse could be entitled to $150,000 or more from your estate. Therefore, you should consider consulting an attorney if you plan to leave your spouse less than the elective share required under Minnesota law.

I/T/F Bank Accounts versus Joint Ownership

One way of keeping bank accounts out of your estate and still retain control is to title them *in trust for* or I/T/F with a named beneficiary. Some banks may use the letters POD for *pay on death*. Stock brokerage accounts may use TOD for *transfer on death*. Either way the result is the same. No one except you can get the money until your death, and on death it immediately goes directly to the person you name, without a will or probate proceeding. These are sometimes called *Totten Trusts* after the court case that declared them legal.

Example: Rich opened a bank account in the name of "Rich, I/T/F Mary." If Rich dies, the money automatically goes to Mary, but prior to his death Mary has no control over the account. She does not even have to know about it, and Rich can take Mary's name off the account at any time.

Securities Registered as I/T/F

The drawback of the Totten Trust has been that it was only good for cash in a bank account. Stocks and bonds still had to go through probate. But now Minnesota allows I/T/F accounts for securities. These can include stocks, bonds, mutual funds, and other similar investments. An estate with cash and securities can pass at death with no need for court proceedings.

To set up your securities to transfer automatically on death you need to have them correctly titled. If you use a brokerage account, the brokerage company should have a form for you to do this.

If your securities are registered in your own name or with your spouse, you may retitle them in TOD format with the designation of your beneficiary. The following are examples of ways to list title to securities.

Sole owner with sole beneficiary:

```
John S Brown TOD John S Brown Jr.
```

Multiple owners with sole beneficiary (John and Mary are joint tenants with right of survivorship and when they die, John, Jr., inherits the property):

```
John S Brown Mary B Brown JT TEN TOD John S
Brown Jr
```

Multiple owners-substituted beneficiary (John and Mary are joint tenants with right of survivorship and when they die John Jr. inherits the property, but if John predeceases them then Peter inherits it):

```
John S Brown Mary B Brown JT TEN TOD John S
Brown Jr SUB BEN Peter Q Brown
```

Multiple owners-lineal descendants (John and Mary are joint tenants with right of survivorship and when they die John, Jr., inherits the property, but if John predeceases them then John, Jr.'s lineal descendants inherit it):

```
John S Brown Mary B Brown JT TEN TOD John S
Brown Jr LDPS
```

WILLS AND YOUR HOMESTEAD

There are two meanings for the word *homestead* in Minnesota. One is the tax exemption that you get from the property appraiser when you reside on a property. This has nothing to do with whether the property is homestead for estate purposes.

A *homestead* for estate purposes is property that is the permanent residence of a legal resident of Minnesota who has a spouse or minor children and who owns the property in his or her name alone.

If your property is homestead your will has no control over it. Upon your death your homestead automatically passes as follows:

- If you have both a spouse and minor children, your spouse gets the right to live in the homestead for the rest of his or her life and your children get it upon your spouse's death.

- If you have a spouse and no minor children, your spouse gets the homestead, no matter what your will says.

- If you have minor children but no spouse, your children get the homestead in equal shares, no matter what your will says.

Whether or not a home is legally a homestead is a tricky legal question. It may depend on which spouse is providing the support or whether or not the property is also being used for business purposes. If you have a question of whether your property is homestead for estate purposes, you should consult a lawyer who is experienced in estate planning.

Because homestead property can only be property which is in individual ownership, jointly held property and property in trust does not come under these rules. To avoid property becoming homestead property, it must be purchased in joint names or in trust. If it is already in an individual's name it cannot be put in trust or in joint ownership without the spouse's signature.

EXEMPTIONS

If you have a spouse or minor children, then up to $10,000 in "household furniture, furnishings, personal property, appliances, and one automobile" in your name are exempt from your will. This is called *exempt property*. If you have a spouse, then your spouse gets this property and if you have no spouse, your children receive it. Additionally, a spouse or minor children may receive a *family allowance* of up to $18,000 a year or $1,500 per month.

Example: Donna dies with a will giving half her property to her husband and half to her grown son from a previous marriage. Donna's property consists of a $5,000 automobile, $5,000 in furniture, and $10,000 in cash. Donna's husband may be able to get the car and the furniture as exempt property and $1,500 per month as a family allowance. Then he and the son would split the remaining money. (The son would get even less if the husband also claimed a *spouse's share* as described on page 7.)

To avoid having property declared exempt it may be specifically given to someone in a will. If certain items are specifically given to certain persons, those items will not be considered part of the exempt property. If cash is kept in a joint or I/T/F bank account it would go to the joint owner or beneficiary and not be used as the family allowance.

Marriage and Your Will

If you get married after making your will and do not rewrite it after the wedding, your spouse gets a share of your estate as if you had no will. This is true unless you have a prenuptial agreement, you made a provision for your spouse in the will, or you stated in the will that you intended not to mention your prospective spouse. (Minn. Stat. Ann., Sec. 524.2-301.)

Example: John made out his will leaving everything to his physically-challenged brother. When he married Joan, an heiress with plenty of money, he didn't change his will because he still wanted his brother to get his estate. When he died, Joan received John's entire estate, and John's brother got nothing.

DIVORCE AND YOUR WILL

A judgment of divorce or annulment automatically changes your will to the effect that the former spouse is treated as if he or she died before the maker of the will. (Minn. Stat. Ann., Secs. 524.2-802.)

NOTE: *A decree of separation does not change your will.*

CHILDREN AND YOUR WILL

If you have a child after making your will and do not rewrite it, the child may receive a share of your estate as if there was no will.

Example: Dave made a will leaving half his estate to his sister and the other half to be shared by his three children. He later has another child and does not revise his will. Upon his death his fourth child would get one quarter of his estate, his sister would get three-eighths and the other three children would each get one-eighth.

It is best to rewrite your will at the birth of a child. However, another solution is to include the following clause after the names of your children in your will.

```
"...and any afterborn children living at the
 time of my death, in equal shares."
```

If you have one or more children and are leaving all of your property to your spouse, then your will would not be affected by the birth of a subsequent child.

YOUR DEBTS

One of the duties of the person administering an estate is to pay the debts of the decedent. Before an estate is distributed, the legitimate debts must be ascertained and paid.

An exception is *secured debts*. These are debts that are protected by a *lien* against property, like a home loan or a car loan. In the case of a secured debt, the loan does not have to be paid before the property is distributed.

Example: John owns a $100,000 house with a $80,000 mortgage and he has $100,000 in the bank. If he leaves the house to his brother and the bank account to his sister, then his brother would receive the home but would owe the $80,000 mortgage.

What if your debts are more than your property? Today, unlike hundreds of years ago, people cannot inherit other peoples' debts. A person's property is used to pay their probate and funeral expenses first, and if there is not enough left to pay their other debts, then the creditors are out of luck. However, if a person leaves property to people and does not have enough assets to pay his or her debts, then the property will be sold to pay the debts.

Example: Jeb's will leaves all of his property to his three children. At the time of his death, Jeb, has $30,000 in medical bills, $11,000 in credit card debt, and his only assets are his car and $5,000 in stock. The car and stock would be sold and the funeral bill and probate fees paid out of the proceeds. If any money was left it would go to the creditors and nothing would be left for the children. The children would not have to pay the medical bills or credit card debt.

ESTATE AND INHERITANCE TAXES

Unlike some states, Minnesota does not have estate or inheritance taxes in most cases. The only time estate taxes would be paid to the state of Minnesota would be if the estate was subject to federal estate taxes and a credit was allowed for state taxes. Then these taxes would be paid to the state and credited against the federal tax due.

There is a federal estate tax for estates above a certain amount. Estates below that amount are allowed a *unified credit,* which exempts them from tax. The unified credit applies to the estate a person can leave at death and to gifts during his or her lifetime. In 2000-2001, the amount exempted by the unified credit is $675,000 but it will rise to $1,000,000 by the year 2006.

Year	Amount
2002-2003	$700,000
2004	$850,000
2005	$950,000
2006	$1,000,000

NOTE: *At the moment, there will be no estate tax in 2010 only, although that could change. It depends on laws that could be passed by the President and Congress.*

ANNUAL EXCLUSION

When a person makes a gift, that gift is subtracted from the amount entitled to the unified credit available to his or her estate at death. However, a person is allowed to make gifts of up to $10,000 per person per year without having these subtracted from the unified credit. This means a married couple can make gifts of up to $20,000 per year. The Taxpayer Relief Act of 1997 provided that this exclusion amount will be adjusted for inflation.

DECIDING IF YOU NEED A MINNESOTA WILL 2

Any person who is eighteen years of age and of sound mind can make a valid·will in Minnesota. Sound mind usually means that you know who are the logical persons that society believes would naturally receive your money and property. This most often means your children and spouse.

NOTE: *Remember that Minnesota law requires that a spouse not be completely disinherited.*

It does not mean you cannot leave your assets to churches, charities or friends. It does not mean that you must give all of your assets to your family. It *does* mean that if this is an area of concern to you it may be prudent to get help from a lawyer as you prepare your will.

Too many lawsuits have been fought over the soundness of someone's mind. Too many estates have been wasted on court battles. Too many wills have not been followed by the court because of lack of evidence of a sound mind. Therefore, it makes sense to prepare your will in a way that the soundness of your mind is clear. The last thing you will want is a costly court fight on the subject, particularly when you're not available to participate.

Most importantly, too many Minnesotans die without leaving a valid will and their wishes are not heeded.

WHAT A WILL CAN DO

A *will* is the legal instrument that allows you to make binding choices about the distribution of your assets upon your death. It is the document, if drawn up according to Minnesota's laws, that makes sure your property is distributed to the people you choose in the way that you choose. It protects your children by allowing you to decide who will care for them and when they will receive your money. And importantly, it allows you to preserve your assets for your loved ones by taking full advantage of the tax laws.

BENEFICIARIES

A will allows you to decide who gets your property after your death. You can give specific personal items to certain persons and choose which of your friends or relatives, if any, deserve a greater share of your estate. You can also leave gifts to schools and charities.

PERSONAL REPRESENTATIVE

A will allows you to decide who will be in charge of handling your estate. This is the person who gathers together all your assets and distributes them to the beneficiaries, hires attorneys or accountants if necessary, and files any essential tax or probate forms.

In Minnesota, this person is called the *personal representative.* (In other states he or she is called the *executor* or *executrix.*) With a will, you can provide that your personal representative does not have to post a surety bond with the court in order to serve and this can save your estate some money. You can also give him or her the power to sell your property and take other actions without getting a court order.

GUARDIAN

A will allows you to choose a guardian for your minor children. This way you can avoid fights among relatives and make sure the best person raises your children. You may also appoint separate guardians over your children and over their money. For example you may appoint your sister as guardian over your children, and your father as guardian over their money. That way, a second person can keep an eye on how the children's money is being spent.

PROTECTING
HEIRS

You can set up a trust to provide that your property is not distributed immediately. Many people feel that their children would not be ready to handle large sums of money at the age of majority, which in most states is eighteen. A will can direct that the money is held until the children are twenty-one, or twenty-five, or older.

MINIMIZING
TAXES

If your estate is over the amount protected by the federal *unified credit* ($675,000 in 2001, but will be rising to $1,000,000 by the year 2006), then it will be subject to federal estate taxes, except in 2010. (see page 20.) If you wish to lower those taxes, for example by making gifts to charities, you can do so through a will. However, such estate planning is beyond the scope of this book and you should consult an estate planning attorney or another book for further information.

IF YOU HAVE NO WILL

If you do not have a will, Minnesota law provides that your property shall be distributed as follows:

- If you leave a spouse and no children, your spouse gets your entire estate.

- If you leave a spouse and children who are all children of your spouse, your spouse gets the entire estate.

- If you leave a spouse and at least one child who is not your spouse's child then your spouse gets the first $150,000 and half of the balance. Your children get equal shares of the other half.

- If you leave no spouse, all of your children get equal shares of your estate.

- If you leave no spouse and no children then your estate would go to the highest persons on the following list who are living:

  • your parents;

- your brothers and sisters, or if dead, their children;

- your grandparents;

- your uncles and aunts or their descendants; and

- next of kin.

● If you leave no relatives, it goes to the State of Minnesota

OUT-OF-STATE WILLS

A will that is valid in another state should be valid to pass property in Minnesota. But a will that disinherits a spouse can cancel a will in Minnesota. Other provisions that break the rules of public policy in Minnesota could also void the will. It would be best to check with an attorney to make sure.

Another advantage to having a Minnesota will is that as a Minnesota resident your estate will pay no state inheritance taxes. If you move to Minnesota but keep your old will, your former state of residence may try to collect taxes on your estate.

Minnesota also allows a will to be *self-proved* so that the witnesses never have to be called in to take an oath. With special self-proving language in your will the witnesses take the oath at the time of signing and never have to be seen again.

Example: George and Barbara left their state and moved to Minnesota, which has no estate or inheritance taxes, but they never made a new will. Upon their deaths their former state of residence tried to collect a tax from their estate because their old wills stated that they were residents of that state.

WHAT A WILL CANNOT DO

A will cannot direct that anything illegal be done and it cannot put unreasonable conditions on a gift. A provision that your daughter gets all of your property if she divorces her husband would be ignored by the court. She would get the property with no conditions attached. However, you can put in conditions that could be honored.

Example: You could give your daughter your lake cabin with the condition that she keep up its gardens.

To be sure they are enforceable you should consult with an attorney.

A will cannot leave money or property to an animal because animals cannot legally own property. If you wish to continue paying for care of an animal after your death, you should leave the funds in trust or to a friend whom you know will care for the animal.

USING A SIMPLE WILL

The wills in this book will pass your property whether your estate is $1,000 or $100,000,000. However, if your estate is over $675,000 (this amount will rise to $1,000,000 by the year 2006) then you might be able to avoid estate taxes by using a trust or other tax-saving device. The larger your estate, the more you can save on estate taxes by doing more complicated planning. If you have a large estate and are concerned about estate taxes, you should consult an estate planning attorney or a book on estate planning.

WHO SHOULD NOT USE A SIMPLE WILL

WILL
CONTEST

If you expect that there may be a fight over your estate or that some-one might contest your will's validity, then you should consult a lawyer. If you leave less than the statutory share of your estate to your spouse or if you leave one or more of your children out of your will, it is likely that someone will contest your will.

COMPLICATED
ESTATES

If you are the beneficiary of a trust or have any complications in your legal relationships, you may need special provisions in your will.

BLIND OR UNABLE
TO WRITE

A person who is blind or who can sign only with an "X" should also con-sult a lawyer about the proper way to make and execute a will.

ESTATES OVER
$675,000

If you expect to have over $675,000 (this amount will rise to $1,000,000 by the year 2006) at the time of your death, you may want to consult with a CPA or tax attorney regarding tax consequences.

CONDITIONS

If you wish to put some sort of conditions or restrictions on the prop-erty you leave, you should consult a lawyer. For example, if you want to leave money to your brother only if he quits smoking, or to a hospital only if they name a wing in your honor, you should consult an attorney to be sure that your conditions are valid.

MAKING A
SIMPLE WILL

3

Minnesota has very specific laws for creating a valid will. If you want your wishes carried out, you need to follow the laws while you prepare your will and execute it. This chapter gives you practical tips that help you cope with many of those laws. You can find a complete set of those laws in Minnesota Statutes Annotated, Chapters 524 and 525. Essential to putting together a simple will is your ability to follow these statutes and the court rulings that have interpreted them. Success can be yours because these laws and court cases give you the correct formula to enable you to dispose of your estate on your own terms.

PARTIES IN YOUR WILL

One of the most enjoyable parts of drawing up your will is the satisfaction you get once you know that people and groups that you want to give your assets to have been safely identified and recorded in your will. Take all the time you need to consider everyone who is now or was important to you and whether it feels right to you to put them in your will.

PEOPLE   When making your will, it is important to clearly identify the persons you name as your beneficiaries. In some families, names differ only by middle initial or by Jr. or Sr. Be sure to check everyone's name before making your will. You can also add your relationship to the beneficiary, and their location such as "my cousin, George Simpson of St. Paul, Minnesota."

ORGANIZATIONS

The same applies to organizations and charities. For example there is more than one group using the words "cancer society" or "heart association" in their name. Be sure to get the full and correct name of the group that you intend to leave your gift.

SPOUSE AND
CHILDREN

It is a good idea to mention your spouse and children in your will even if you do not leave them any property. That is to show that you are of sound mind and know who are your heirs. As mentioned earlier, if you have a spouse and/or children and plan to leave your property to persons other than them, you should consult an attorney to be sure that your will will be enforceable.

SPECIAL GIFTS OF PERSONAL PROPERTY

Because people acquire and dispose of personal property so often, it is not advisable to list a lot of small items in your will. Otherwise, when you sell or replace one of them you may have to rewrite your will.

One solution is to describe the type of item you wish to give. For example, instead of saying, "I leave my 2000 Ford to my sister," you should say, "I leave any automobile I own at the time of my death to my sister."

Of course, if you do mean to give a specific item you should describe it. For example instead of "I leave my diamond ring to Joan," you should say, "I leave to Joan the one-half carat diamond ring that I inherited from my grandmother," because you might own more than one diamond ring at the time of your death.

HANDWRITTEN
LIST OF
PERSONAL
PROPERTY

In Minnesota, you are allowed to have a written statement or list of items to be distributed upon your death. The only items you cannot have distributed this way are money, coin collections, and property used in a trade or business.

You may list these special gift items in the body of the will, what they are and to whom they go or you can make a separate writing with those items and the recipients. If you put into the will itself the items and who gets them, then every time you change your mind you have to amend your will or draw up a new one.

To make a separate writing legal, you must refer to this separate written list in your will as being in existence at the time of your death. It must be either in your handwriting or signed by you, and it must describe the items and the intended recipients with "reasonable certainty."

One example of what is meant by reasonable certainty is "my 48 inch string of pearls goes to my niece Elizabeth R. Windsor of New London, Connecticut." Another is "my Elvis records go to my next door neighbor Jon Lenin". A third is "my antique fishing rods go to the Duluth Fishing Museum." Keep in mind that you are writing for people who may not be as familiar with your possessions as you are. Also, you do not want the recipients you name to get mixed up with anyone else.

The separate writing may be prepared before or after you sign, date and have your will witnessed. You may change it any time and you do not have to have it witnessed. The wills in this book include a clause stating that you may leave such a writing. This book also has a form, PREFERENCES LIST that is specifically for this purpose. (see form 2, p.77.)

You can have more than one writing, but if you leave an item to more than one person, the most recent writing will control the distribution of the item. (Minn. Stat. Ann., Sec. 524.2-513.)

If you give a copy of the list to everyone concerned it will help reduce surprises, confusion and possible friction in the family. Of course, anytime you change that list, you need to remember to give out the new list.

NOTE: *Section 663 of the Internal Revenue Code excludes specific bequests of tangible personal property from the estate for tax purposes. If your estate is over $675,000 (this amount will rise to $1,000,000 by the year 2006) you may want to consult a tax advisor about taking advantage of this provision.*

SPECIFIC BEQUESTS

Occasionally a person will want to leave a little something to a friend or charity and the rest to the family. This can be done with a *specific bequest* such as "$1,000 to my dear friend Martha Jones." Of course there could be a problem if, at the time of a person's death, there was not anything left after the specific bequests.

Example: At the time of making his will, Todd had $1,000,000 in assets. He felt generous so he left $50,000 to a local hospital, $50,000 to a local group that took care of homeless animals, and the rest to his children. Unfortunately, several years later, the stock market crashed and he committed suicide by jumping off a bridge. His estate at the time was worth only $110,000 so after the above specific bequests, the legal fees, and expenses of probate, there was nothing left for his five children.

Another problem with specific bequests is that some of the property may be worth considerably more or less at death than when the will was made.

Example: Joe wanted his two children to equally share his estate. His will left his son his stocks (worth $500,000 at the time) and his daughter $500,000 in cash. By the time of Joe's death the stock was only worth $100,000.

He should have left "fifty percent" of his estate to each child. If giving certain things to certain people is an important part of your estate plan, you can give specific items to specific persons, but remember to make changes if your assets change.

JOINT BENEFICIARIES

Be careful about leaving one item of personal property to more than one person. For example, if you leave something to your son and his wife, what would happen if they divorce? Even if you leave something to two of your own children, what if they cannot agree about who will have possession of it? Whenever possible, leave property to one person.

REMAINDER CLAUSE

One of the most important clauses in a will is the *remainder clause*. This is the clause that says something like "all the rest of my property I leave to…" This clause makes sure that the will disposes of all property owned at the time of death and that nothing is forgotten.

In a simple will the best way to distribute property is to put it all in the remainder clause. In the example with Todd in the previous section on page 24, the problem would have been avoided if the will had read as follows: "The rest, residue, and remainder of my estate I leave, five percent to ABC Hospital, five percent to XYZ Animal Welfare League, and ninety percent to be divided equally among my children…"

ALTERNATE BENEFICIARIES

You should always provide for an *alternate beneficiary* in case the person you name dies before you and you do not have a chance to make out a new will.

SURVIVOR OR
DESCENDANTS

Suppose your will leaves your property to your sister and brother but your brother dies before you. Should his share go to your sister or to your brother's children or grandchildren?

If you are giving property to two or more persons and if you want it all to go to the other if one of them dies, then you would specify "or the survivor of them."

If, on the other hand, you want the property to go to the children of the deceased person you should state in your will, "or their lineal descendants." This would include his or her children and grandchildren.

FAMILY OR
PERSON

If you decide you want the property to go to your brother's children and grandchildren, you must next decide if an equal share should go to each family or to each person.

Example: If your brother leaves three grandchildren, and one is an only child of his daughter and the others are the children of his son, should all grandchildren get equal shares, or should they take their parent's share?

When you want each family to get an equal share it is called *per stirpes*. When you want each person to get an equal share it is called *per capita*. Most of the wills in this book use per stirpes because that is the most common way property is left. If you wish to leave your property per capita then you can rewrite the will with this change.

Example: Alice leaves her property to her two daughters, Mary and Pat in equal shares, or to their lineal descendants per stirpes. Both daughters die before Alice. Mary leaves one child; Pat leaves two children. In this case Mary's child would get half of the estate and Pat's children would split the other half of the estate. If Alice had specified per capita instead of per stirpes then each child would have gotten one-third of the estate.

Per Stirpes Distribution

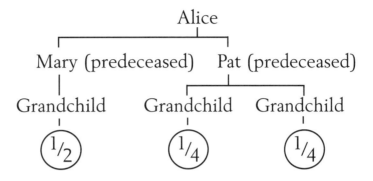

Per Capita Distribution

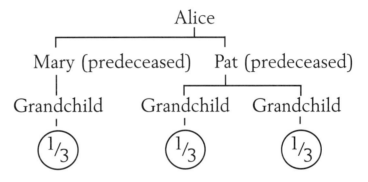

There are fourteen different will forms in this book that should cover the options most people want, but you may want to divide your property slightly differently from what is stated in these forms. If so, you can retype the forms according to these rules, specifying whether the property should go to the survivor or the lineal descendants. If this is confusing to you, you should consider seeking the advice of an attorney.

SURVIVORSHIP

Many people put a clause in their will stating that anyone receiving property under the will must survive for thirty days (or forty-five or sixty) after the death of the person who made the will. This is so that if the two people die in the same accident there will not be two probates and the property will not go to the other party's heirs.

Example: Fred and Wilma were married and each had children by previous marriages. They did not have survivorship clauses in their wills and they were in an airplane crash and died. Fred's children hired several expert witnesses and a large law firm to prove that at the time of the crash Fred lived for a few minutes longer than Wilma. That way, when Wilma died first, all of her property went to Fred. When he died a few minutes later, all of Fred *and* Wilma's property went to his children. Wilma's children got nothing.

GUARDIANS

If you have minor children you should name a guardian for them. There are two types of guardians, a guardian over the *person* and a guardian over the *property*. The first is the person who decides where the children will live and makes the other parental decisions for them. A guardian of the property is in charge of the minor's property and inheritance. In most cases, one person is appointed guardian of both the person and property. But some people prefer the children to live with one person, but to have the money held by another person. (Minn. Stat. Ann., Sec. 525.6155.)

Example: Sandra was a widow with a young daughter. She knew that if anything happened to her, her sister would be the best person to raise her daughter. But her sister was never good with money. So when Sandra made out her will, she named her sister as guardian over the person of her daughter and she named her father as guardian over the estate of her daughter.

When naming a guardian, it is always advisable to name an alternate guardian in case your first choice is unable to serve for any reason.

CHILDREN'S TRUST

When a parent dies leaving a minor child and the child's property is held by a guardian, the guardianship ends when the child reaches the age of eighteen, and all of the property is turned over to the child. Most parents do not feel their children are competent at the age of eighteen to handle large sums of money and prefer that it be held until the child is twenty-one, twenty-five, thirty, or even older.

If you wish to set up a complicated system of determining when your children should receive various amounts of your estate, or if you want the property held to a higher age than thirty-five, you should consult a lawyer to draft a trust. However, if you want a simple provision that the funds be held until they reach a higher age than eighteen, and you have someone you trust to make decisions about paying for education or other expenses for your child or children, you can put that provision in your will as a children's trust.

The children's trust trustee can be the same person as the guardian or a different person. It is advisable to name an alternate trustee if your first choice is unable to handle it.

PERSONAL REPRESENTATIVE

A *personal representative* is the person who will be in charge of your probate. He or she will gather your assets, handle the sale of them if necessary, prepare an inventory, hire an attorney, and distribute the property. This should be a person you trust, and if it is, then you can state in your will that no bond will be required to be posted by him or her. Otherwise the court will require that a surety bond be paid for by your estate to guaranty that the person is honest. You can appoint a bank to handle your estate, but their fees are usually very high.

It is best to appoint a resident of your state, both because it is easier and because a bond may be required of a non-resident even if your will waives it.

MULTIPLE APPOINTEES
Some people like to name two persons to handle their estate to avoid jealousy, or to have them check on each other's honesty. However, this is not a good idea. It makes double work in getting the papers signed, and there can be problems if they cannot agree on something.

FEES
You may put in your will how much you want paid to the person who handles your estate. A close friend or family member may refuse to be paid. But if there is a lot of work involved, that person may ask for the fee. Some family members may insist that the person doing the work be paid. If no reasonable amount is listed in your will, a personal representative might be able to go to court and ask for payment for services rendered. (Minn. Stat. Ann., Sec. 534.3-719.)

SELLING REAL ESTATE
In Minnesota, a personal representative cannot sell real estate without approval by the court unless the power to do so is included in the will. If you trust your personal representative you can avoid the expense and delay of this by giving him or her the power to do so without court approval.

WITNESSES

A will must be witnessed by at least two persons to be valid. In all other states, except Vermont, only two witnesses are required. Unless you own property in Vermont, you do not need more than two witnesses.

In Minnesota (unlike some states), it is legal for a beneficiary of a will to be a witness to the will. However, this is not a good idea, especially if there is anyone who might go to court to fight your will.

SELF-PROVING AFFIDAVIT

As mentioned above, a will only needs two witnesses to be legal, but if it includes a self-proving clause and is notarized, then the will can be admitted to probate quickly and there is no need to contact the witnesses. If it is not self-proved, then one of the witnesses must go to the courthouse and sign a statement that the will is genuine.

In an emergency situation, for example, if you are bedridden and there is no notary available, you can execute your will without the self-proving page. As long as it has two witnesses it will be valid. The only drawback is that the witnesses will later have to sign an oath.

DISINHERITING SOMEONE

Because it may result in your will being challenged in court, you should not make your own will if you intend to disinherit someone. However, you may wish to leave one child less than another because you already made a gift to that child, or perhaps that child needs the money less than the other.

If you do give more to one child than to another, then you should state your reasons to show that you thought out your plan. Otherwise the one who received less might argue that you did not realize what you were doing and were not competent to make a will.

FUNERAL ARRANGEMENTS

There is no harm in stating your preferences in your will, but in most states, directions for a funeral are not legally enforceable. Often a will is not found until after the funeral. Therefore it is better to tell your family about your wishes or to make prior arrangements yourself.

If you are a veteran, make sure your discharge papers are kept where they can be quickly found. Most National Cemeteries, including Fort Snelling, require that honorable discharge papers be presented to them before burial arrangements can be made.

HANDWRITTEN WILLS

In some states a person can hand write a will, without any witnesses, and it will be held valid. This is called a *holographic* will. In Minnesota such a will is not valid. Handwritten wills or wills not witnessed by two people according to the requirements in Minnesota will guarantee that the will cannot be honored.

FORMS

There are fourteen different will forms included in this book for easy use. You can either tear them out, or photocopy them, or you can retype them on plain paper.

If you photocopy the forms on separate pages or type your will on more than one piece of paper, you should staple the pages together, initial each page, and have both witnesses initial each page. Each page should state at the bottom, "page 1 of 3," "page 2 of 3," etc.

CORRECTIONS

Your will should have no white-outs or erasures. If for some reason it is impossible to make a will without corrections, they should be initialed by you and both witnesses. You may instead want to make a new will to prevent the will from being invalid. You may want to make changes, however. The best way to make changes, rather than make a new will, is to make a *codicil*. (see pages 36-37.)

EXECUTING YOUR WILL 4

The signing of a will is a serious legal event and must be done properly or the will may be declared invalid. Preferably, it should be done in a private room without distraction.

To be properly executed under Minnesota law your will must conform to these rules. (Minn. Stat. Ann., Secs. 524.2-502.)

- It must be written down.
  - You can put your will on a typewriter.
  - You can put your will on a word processor and print it out.
  - You can dictate your will to someone who will type it or put it on a word processor and print it out.

- **Under no circumstances can your will be oral, in handwriting, or only on video or audiotape.**

- It must be signed by you or in your name by some other individual in your conscious presence and at your direction.

- It also must be signed by at least two people, each of whom signs within a reasonable time after they witness either:
  - your signing of the will; or
  - your acknowledgment of your signature; or
  - your acknowledgement of your will.

PROCEDURE

To be sure your will is valid, you should follow these rules:

- State to your witnesses: "This is my will. I have read it and I understand it and this is how I want it to read. I want you two (or three) people to be my witnesses." Contrary to popular belief, you do not have to read it to the witnesses nor do you have to let them read it.

- You must date your will and sign your name at the end in ink, exactly as it is printed in the will, and you should initial each page as all witnesses watch.

- You and the other witnesses should watch as each witness signs in ink and initials each page.

- Number each page and write that it is "page 1 of 1," "page 1 of 2," "page 4 of 5," and so forth.

SELF-PROVING AFFIDAVIT

As explained in Chapter 3, it is important to attach a self-proving affidavit to your will. This means that you will need to have a notary public present to watch everyone sign. If it is impossible to have a notary present, your will will still be valid, but the probate process may be delayed.

After your witnesses have signed as attesting witnesses under your name, you and they should sign the self-proving page and the notary should notarize it. The notary should not be one of your witnesses.

It is a good idea to make at least one copy of your will, but you should not personally sign the copies or have them notarized. The reason for this is if you cancel or destroy your will someone may produce a copy and have it probated, or if you lose or destroy a copy a court may assume you intended to revoke the original.

Example: Michael typed out a copy of his will and made two photocopies. He had the original and both copies signed and notarized. He then gave the original to his sister who was his personal representative and kept the two copies. Upon his death the two copies were not found among his papers. Because these copies were in his possession and not found it was assumed that he destroyed them. A court ruled that by destroying them he must have intended to revoke the original will and his property went to persons not listed in his will.

AFTER SIGNING YOUR WILL 5

Even though you have finished putting your will together, there are a few more things to think about. You need to keep it someplace safe. You may even change it. And if your situation changes as months and years go by, you may really need to change it. Minnesota Statutes Annotated, Sections 524.2-507, 508 and 509 and case law allow you the flexibility to change your will whenever you want. However, to keep your will valid, you must follow the rules they have established. This chapter highlights some of the most important points in those rules.

STORING YOUR WILL

Your will should be kept in a place safe from fire and easily accessible to your heirs. Your personal representative should know of its whereabouts. It can be kept in a home safe, fire box, or safe deposit box..

In some states the opening of a safe deposit box in a bank after a person's death is a complicated affair, but in Minnesota, a will can be removed from a safe deposit box easily, so you can keep it there.

If you are close to your children and can trust them explicitly, then you could allow one of them to keep the will in his or her safe deposit box. However, if you later decide to limit that child's share there could be a problem.

Example: Diane made out her will giving her property to her two children equally and gave it to her older child, Bill, to hold. Years later, Bill moved away and her younger child, Mary, took care of her by coming over every day. Diane made a new will giving most her property to Mary. Upon Diane's death Bill came to town and found the new will in Diane's house, but he destroyed it and probated the old will that gave him half the property.

REVOKING YOUR WILL

The usual way to revoke a will is to execute a new one that states that it revokes all previously made wills. To revoke a will without making a new one, one can tear, burn, cancel, deface, obliterate, or destroy it, as long as this is done with the intention of revoking it. If this is done accidentally, the will is not legally revoked.

Example: Ralph tells his son Clyde to go to the basement safe and tear up his (Ralph's) will. If Clyde does not tear it up in Ralph's presence, it is probably not effectively revoked.

REVIVAL What if you change your will by drafting a new one, and later decide you do not like the changes and want to go back to your old will? Can you destroy the new one and revive the old one? NO! Once you execute a new will revoking an old will, you cannot revive the old will unless you execute a new document stating that you intend to revive the old will. In other words, you really should execute a new will.

CHANGING YOUR WILL

You should not make any changes on your will after it has been signed. If you cross out a person's name or add a clause to a will that has already been signed, your change will not be valid and your entire will might become invalid.

One way to amend a will is to execute a *codicil.* A codicil is an amendment to a will. However, a codicil must be executed just like a will. It must have the same number of witnesses, and to be self-proved it must include a self-proving page that must be notarized.

Because a codicil requires the same formality as a will, it is usually better to just make a new will.

In an emergency situation, if you want to change something in your will, but cannot get to a notary to have it self-proved, you can execute a codicil which is witnessed, but not self-proved. As long as it is properly witnessed (two witnesses) it will legally change your will. The only drawback would be that the witnesses would have to later sign an oath if it were not self-proved.

To prepare a CODICIL TO WILL, use form 18. (see form 18, p.109.) To self-prove the codicil, use SELF-PROVED CODICIL AFFIDAVIT. (see form 19, p.111.)

MAKING A HEALTH CARE DIRECTIVE

6

In Minnesota, a **HEALTH CARE DIRECTIVE** has replaced the *living will* and the *health care power of attorney*. A health care directive is a combination of these two old-style documents. (Minn. Stat. Ann., Sec. 145C.) In 1998, the State decided it was time to make things easier for people who want to have a legal document to protect their wishes for what health care they want at the end of life.

A **HEALTH CARE DIRECTIVE** allows you to do several things. (see form 20, p.113.) In it, you may describe the exact treatments that you do, or do not, want. You may include your instructions on whether you want artificially administered nutrition or hydration. The directives most likely to carry out your wishes will have specific instructions appropriate for your condition.

The **HEALTH CARE DIRECTIVE** allows you to choose a person to make health decisions for you when you are no longer able to make them. This person is called your *health care agent*. Appointment of an agent is an option; it is **not** something you are required to do. It allows you to pick a person you trust to make decisions based on what you have in your written instructions or what you have told them. If you have not made your wishes known, your agent is required to act in your best interest.

WHO CAN MAKE
A HEALTH CARE DIRECTIVE

Any person who is eighteen years of age and of sound mind can make a valid HEALTH CARE DIRECTIVE. Young people who have illnesses or have been in an accident can become incompetent to make or communicate their wishes just as well as older folks can.

WHY YOU SHOULD WRITE
A HEALTH CARE DIRECTIVE

A HEALTH CARE DIRECTIVE helps you to live the end of your life and your dying process the way you want to. If you cannot communicate your decisions, it lets someone you trust see to it that actions taken for you are based on your wishes, and no one else's. If you do not want certain things done for you, it allows you to have those things written out clearly, so that there are no mistakes about what you really want. Even if you can communicate, you can still have a directive and enjoy its benefits. To do this, you must put it in your directive that you want it to take effect before you become incapacitated.

Your health care directive will become a legally enforceable document when you have signed and dated it and two people or a notary have witnessed it. Neither the notary nor either of the witnesses can be your health care agent. If you want a health care provider or one of its employees to be your agent, explain why in the directive.

WHEN TO MAKE A DIRECTIVE

The time to make a directive is before you need it and while you have plenty of time to think clearly. As long as you have the capacity to make your own health care decisions and to get fully informed about your condition and treatment options, you have the complete legal and moral right to make all health care decisions for yourself. By making a directive in advance of the time when you might need it, you extend this opportunity.

The law does not require you to have an advance directive. If you do not have one and you become incapacitated, your family and physicians will have to make those decisions without your input. A HEALTH CARE DIRECTIVE can help avoid family conflict, guilt feelings, anxieties and uncertainties about your treatment, or lack of it. If making these decisions in your culture is a family matter, the preparation of an advance directive gives you the chance to involve everyone who should be part of the decision-making.

PREPARING A DIRECTIVE

Focus on what it is that you really and truly desire. Consider your beliefs. Think about your values. Contemplate your philosophy about living and dying. Ponder what it is exactly that you want done for you. The process of preparing this document gives you the opportunity to discuss matters with your family, friends, clergy and physicians. Your health care providers can help you to understand what treatments are available and which ones you do or do not want. It can give you peace of mind and confidence that things will be done your way, if you can no longer communicate to others what that way is.

Above all, you must put together a treatment plan with your physician. There is no getting around it that for most people their physicians are the most knowledgeable people about medical conditions and treatment options. They are the ones who can help you to identify the specific, relevant instructions for your condition that you put into your directive. They are also the ones who most often will be in the position to affect your end of life treatment. Make your physician one of your essential partners in deciding the medical actions that are taken for you.

A HEALTH CARE DIRECTIVE made well in advance gives you all the time you need to consider what it is in life and in the dying process that is of importance to you and to your family. It gives you freedom to contemplate these matters when you have the mental capacity to do so. You have the opportunity to learn about and acquire an understanding of the nature and consequences of the decisions that you make.

PREPARATION Ask yourself:

- Why do I want to have a directive?

- What do I value about health and health care?

- Who do I trust to make my decisions when I can't and communicate my wishes when I am no longer able?

Talk with others.

- Ask your physician and all others who provide you with health care about your options for care and tell them you are preparing a directive.

- Tell your family, friends and clergy what you are doing.

- Make everyone understand what it is that you want.

- If you choose to have a health care agent, ask each one if they are willing to serve, discuss your wishes thoroughly with each of them. If you do not want them to have access to your medical records let them know that and put that in your directive.

Write out your specific instructions (see form 20 in Appendix C).

- Write about your important values, your goals, your beliefs, your concerns and your fears.

- Write your wishes for what is to be done in specific medical situations.

- Put in the directive anything else you want your family, agent and health care providers to know, and then talk over all of these matters with them.

Give your directive to:

- all health care providers, including your physician, for your medical records;

- your family, clergy, your health care agent and that person's back up;

- nursing homes, hospice and home care agencies; and

- anyone else who is involved with your with care.

Review your directive regularly.

- Are the instructions in your directive still what you want done?

- Discuss the directive and its contents with your physician, family, health care agent and back up agent. Make sure each one still understands what it is that you want.

- Change, update and give copies of your latest version to all the appropriate people whenever you need to.

A HEALTH CARE DIRECTIVE is a significant document for your peace of mind. Prepare it according to Minnesota law so that you can make it the legally binding document that you want. (Minn. Stat. Ann., Sec. 145C.05.) Use form 20 in Appendix C to help you get started.

STORING THE HEALTH CARE DIRECTIVE

First, the original directive (signed, dated, and witnessed by two people or a notary) needs to be kept in a safe but very accessible place. Do not keep it with your will. Second, the directive must be available to everyone who will need it to carry out your wishes. Third, make sure it is in every medical record that you have. Every time you go into your doctor's office, make sure it's in your chart. Every time you are hospitalized or go into a hospice, make sure in it's your records. This may sound like a lot of work, but health care directives can get misplaced. So, you want to take responsibility to ensure that it is where it needs to be, when it needs to be there for you.

Make sure that your nursing home and your home health care agency have copies. Also, give copies to your family, friends, clergy and anyone who might be caring for you.

Be sure to give a copy to your health care agent and the back up person who you ask to fill in as health care agent, if the first person cannot. If the first person is out of town or ill when you need them, or cannot be reached for any reason, you really will be best served if you have a backup. It is much easier for most people to say yes to make decisions on your behalf if they have clear, written directions from you. If you are having trouble deciding whom to appoint as your health care agent, you may want to ask your attorney for some thoughts.

CHANGING THE DIRECTIVE

You may change your directive as often as you want. Each time you do, you have to follow some formalities. You can either:

1) execute another one (write out your instructions, sign, date and have it witnessed by two people or a notary); or

2) destroy the original; or

3) execute a written statement that says the previous directive is revoked; or,

4) if you do not want to have one anymore, state your intent to revoke it in the presence of two witnesses. These witnesses do not have to be in the presence of each other.

Once you do make changes, you have to be sure everyone who should know about your changes, gets your message. You should review your directive every so often to be sure that what you wrote the first time is still what you want.

A HEALTH CARE DIRECTIVE is an important legal document. If there is anything in this book about health care directives that you are unsure of (including form 20 in Appendix C to help you make your own directive), ask a legal professional to help you understand it fully. If needed, ask that person to help you fill it out properly and according to the way you want things done.

Making Anatomical Gifts

7

Minnesota residents who are at least 18 years of age or a minor with the written consent of a parent or legal guardian are allowed to donate their bodies or organs for research or transplantation. Consent may be given by a relative of the deceased person, but because relatives are often in shock or too upset to make such a decision, it is better to have one's intent made clear before death.

You can do this by putting a statement in your will or health care directive. You also can have it imprinted on your Minnesota Driver's License. But, if you do not have a drivers license and you instead use an Official State Picture I.D. you <u>cannot</u> put it on that. Even if your driver's license has been revoked, suspended, has expired, or canceled, it will not invalidate your gift.

The gift may be of all or part of one's body, and it may be made to a specific person such as a physician or an ill relative or friend.

The document making the donation must be signed. If the donor cannot sign, then the document may be signed for him at his direction in the presence of the witnesses and the document must state that it has been signed. (Minn. Stat. Ann., Sec. 525.9211.)

The donor may designate in the document who the physician is that will carry out the procedure.

You may change or revoke your anatomical gift *only* by:

- a signed statement;

- an oral statement made in the presence of two people;

- any form of communication during a terminal illness or injury to a health care professional or member of the clergy; or,

- delivery of a signed statement to a specified recipient who has already received your signed document telling of your gift.

If you make the gift in your will or HEALTH CARE DIRECTIVE, you may want to amend or revoke them. But this is not required. You can use any one of the four ways listed to make the changes.

You do not ever have to make an anatomical gift. If you think that you have to make your feelings known that you do not want to make such a gift, all you have to do is put your refusal in writing and sign it. If you have a terminal illness or injury, you do not have to put your refusal in writing, but you to have to communicate it to a health care professional or member of the clergy.

You may want to make an anatomical gift but do not want it on your driver's license, in your HEALTH CARE DIRECTIVE, or will. If that is the case, you may use the ORGAN DONOR CARD included in Appendix C. (see form 21, p.120.)

SUMMARY OF WILLS 8

If you care about what happens to your property after you are gone, you need to have a valid will drawn up. You may find that putting together a will is an emotional and thought intensive task. This book has the tools you need to meet these challenges. Whether you do all the work yourself or get professional assistance, your reward for getting it done is great. You can achieve valuable peace of mind about this important part of your existence and that of your loved ones.

Minnesota makes the laws that control preparation of a will. You must follow these laws to achieve your goals. After all the work you put into making your will it could be tragic for your loved ones if a court disregards your wishes. You may want to go back and review the basic rules to determine if you have any more questions about such things as how joint tenancy affects probate and your will. Perhaps you want to think more about other tools that allow property to pass without a will, such as pay on death accounts.

You may have a need to review Minnesota's laws about spousal share. In Minnesota it is against public policy to disinherit a spouse. One reason is because the surviving spouse may have children to raise. Also, Minnesota believes that is important to keep surviving spouses and dependents off public welfare.

Your situation may be complicated and a simple will does not fulfill your needs. For example, if you decide you need a trust, you will need a lawyer to help you put that in place. Perhaps you do not feel up to the task and would feel more confident if you get the help of legal and financial professionals to complete your simple will. Review areas in the book that point out where it might be appropriate for you to use the services of others.

As you have discovered, there are many matters to contemplate in the will-making process. Some of these include:

- the people and organizations you want to be beneficiaries;

- specific bequests of money or personal items;

- guardians for your children;

- your personal representative;

- organ donation; and

- funeral arrangements.

The formalities of the paper work are very important. Remember that you cannot have a handwritten will or audio or videotaped one—they just will not hold up in Minnesota. And be sure that you and your witnesses sign it. Also, store it in a safe place. Do not forget to tell someone where it is. Even after you have gone through the whole process of putting together your simple will, you can still change it.

Warning: Follow the rules for changing a will in Chapter 5.

A **HEALTH CARE DIRECTIVE** is a great tool to help you make end of life decisions while you are still able. Remember to share your Directive with your family, friends and health care provider. Keep it up to date with you thoughts and feelings on the subject.

Many people of all ages and cultures feel that it is emotionally difficult to consider making a will. Sometimes, people put off making one until it is too late. If you die without a valid will you may visit hardship on your loved ones. Hopefully this book helped you find what you need to help you to get moving and avoid those unhappy consequences—all the best as you put together your simple will.

GLOSSARY

A

administrator. A person appointed by the court to oversee distribution of the property of someone who died (either without a will, or if the person designated in the will is unable to serve). Another word sometimes used for personal representative.

attested will. A will that includes an attestation clause and has been signed in front of witnesses.

B

beneficiary. A person who is entitled to receive property from a person who died (regardless of whether there is a will).

bequest. Personal property left to someone in a will.

C

children's trust. A trust set up to hold property given to children. Usually it provides that the children will not receive their property until they reach a higher age than the age of majority.

codicil. An amendment to a will.

community property. Property acquired by a husband and wife by their labors during their marriage.

D

decedent. A person who has died.

descendent. A child, grandchild, great-grandchild, etc.

devise. Real property, such as the family residence, any type of land, a lake cabin, a family farm or other real estate. A person who is entitled to such property is called a *devisee*.

donee. The person or facility who receives the gift of an organ.

E

elective share. The portion of the estate which may be taken by a surviving spouse, regardless of what the will says.

estate. All of the property of the person who makes the will.

executor (*executrix* if female). A person appointed in a will to oversee distribution of the property of someone who died with a will. However, in Florida today, this person is called a *personal representative*.

exempt property. Property that is exempt from distribution as a normal part of the estate.

F

family allowance. An amount of money set aside from the estate to support the family of the decedent for a period of time.

H

health care. Any care, treatment, service, or procedure to maintain, diagnose, or otherwise affect a person's physical or mental condition. It includes the provision of nutrition, parenteral hydration (IV's) or breathing tube. It also includes the establishment of a person's abode within or without Minnesota and personal security safeguards for a person, to the extent decisions on these matters relate to the health care needs of the person.

heir. A person who will inherit from a decedent who died without a will.

holographic will. A will in which all of the material provisions are entirely in the handwriting of the maker. Holographic wills are *not* legal in Minnesota.

homestead. A person's permanent legal residence located in Minnesota.

I

intestate. Without making a will. One who dies without a will is said to have *died intestate*.

intestate share. The portion of the estate a spouse is entitled to receive if there is no will.

J

joint tenancy. A type of property ownership by two or more persons, in which if one owner dies, that owner's interest goes to the other joint tenants (not to the deceased owner's heirs as in tenancy in common).

L

legacy. Real property left to someone in a will. A person who is entitled to a legacy is called a *legatee*.

living will. A document expressing the writer's desires regarding how medical care is to be handled in the event the writer is not able to express his or her wishes concerning the use of life-prolonging medical procedures.

P

per capita. Distribution of property with equal shares going to each person.

per stirpes. Distribution of property with equal shares going to each family line.

personal representative. A person appointed by the court, or will, to oversee distribution of the property of the person who died. This is a more modern term than "administrator," "executor," etc., and applies regardless of whether there is a will.

probate. The process of settling a decedent's estate through the probate court.

R

residue. The property that is left over in an estate after all specific bequests and devises.

S

self-proving affidavit. A form added to a will in which the will maker and witnesses state under oath that they have signed and witnessed the will.

special gift, specific bequest *or* **specific devise**. A gift in a will of a specific item of property or of a specific amount of cash.

statutory will. A will which has been prepared according to the requirements of a statute.

T

tenancy in common. Ownership of property by two or more people, in which each owner's share would descend to that owner's heirs (not to the other owners as in joint tenancy).

testate. With a will. One who dies with a will is said to have *died testate*.

testator. A person who makes his or her will.

W

will. Includes any codicil and any testamentary instrument that appoints a personal representative or revokes or revises another will.

Appendix A
Internet Sites

If you have access to the Internet, this appendix is for you. The State of Minnesota relies heavily on its statutes to govern wills, anatomical gifts, and health care directives. This appendix lists sites for how you can find those laws.

Internet Sites

A good search engine that can link you to many law and law-related sites for the state of Minnesota is:

http://www.lawmoose.com

Wills

http://www.revisor.leg.state.mn.us/stats/524

http://www.revisor.leg.state.mn.us/stats/525

Health Care Directives

http://www.revisor.leg.state.mn.us/stats/145C

http://www.revisor.leg.state.mn.us/stats/149A.80

http://www.revisor.leg.state.mn.us/stats/253.B.03 and .04

http://www.revisor.leg.state.mn.us/stats/525.544 and .921to .9224

ANATOMICAL GIFT OF AN ORGAN

http://www.revisor.leg.state.mn.us/stats/525.921 to 525.9224

APPENDIX B
SAMPLE FILLED-IN FORMS

The following pages include sample filled-in forms for some of the wills in Appendix C. They are filled out in different ways for different situations. You should look at all of them to see how the different sections can be filled in. Only one example of a SELF-PROVED WILL AFFIDAVIT is shown, but you should use it with every will.

Last Will and Testament

I, _____John Smith_____ a resident of _____Dakota_____ County, Minnesota do hereby make, publish, and declare this to be my Last Will and Testament, hereby revoking any and all Wills and Codicils heretofore made by me.

FIRST: I direct that all my valid debts and funeral expenses be paid out of my estate as soon after my death as is practicable.

SECOND: I make the following special gifts:

If I have made one of more written lists which have been signed by me, and dated, and otherwise prepared in accordance with the Minnesota law M.S.A. Section 524.2-513, then I give the property described in such list or lists to the person or persons named in such list(s) who survive me. I give all tangible personal property not effectively distributed by the provisions of any such written list to: _____

THIRD: I give, devise, and bequeath all my estate, real, personal, and mixed, of whatever kind and wherever situated, of which I may die seized or possessed, or in which I may have any interest or over which I may have any power of appointment or testamentary disposition, to my spouse, _____Barbara Smith_____. If my said spouse does not survive me, I give, and bequeath the said property to _____my sisters, Jan Smith, Joan Smith, and Jennifer Smith in equal shares------------

_____,
or the survivor of them.

FOURTH: In the event that any beneficiary fails to survive me by thirty days, then this will shall take effect as if that person had predeceased me.

FIFTH: I hereby nominate, constitute, and appoint _____Barbara Smith_____ as Personal Representative of this, my Last Will and Testament. In the event that such named person is unable or unwilling to serve at any time or for any reason, then I nominate, constitute, and appoint _____Reginald Smith_____ as Personal Representative in the place and stead of the person first named herein. It is my will and I direct that my Personal Representative shall not be required to furnish a bond for the faithful performance of his or her duties in any jurisdiction, any provision of law to the contrary notwithstanding, and I give my Personal Representative full power to administer my estate, including the power to settle claims, pay debts, and sell, lease or exchange real and personal property without court order.

I, _____John Smith_____ the testator, sign my name to this instrument this _29th_ day of _____January 2002_____, and being first duly sworn, do hereby declare to the undersigned authority that I sign and execute this instrument as my will and that

1) I sign it willingly
    or

Page ___ of ___

2) IF RELEVANT TO YOUR SITUATION: I willingly direct another to sign for me,

and that I execute it as my free and voluntary act for the purposes therein expressed, and that I am 18 years of age or older, of sound mind, and under no constraint or undue influence.

John Smith
_____
Testator

We, <u>Jane Doe, John Doe</u>_____, the witnesses, sign our names to this instrument, being first duly sworn, and do hereby declare to the undersigned authority that the testator signs and executes this instrument as the testator's will and that the testator

1) signs it willingly
or
2) IF RELEVANT TO YOUR SITUATION: willingly directs another to sign for the testator

and that each of us, in the presence and hearing of the testator, hereby signs this will as witness to the testator's signing, and that to the best of our knowledge the testator is 18 years of age or older, of sound mind, and under no constraint or undue influence.

Jane Doe
_____
Witness

John Doe
_____
Witness

State of <u>Minnesota</u>
County of <u>Dakota</u>

Subscribed, sworn to, and acknowledged before me by <u>John Smith</u>, the testator, and subscribed and sworn to before me by <u>Jane Doe</u>, and <u>John Doe</u>, Witnesses, this <u>29th</u> day of <u>January 2002</u>.
(Notary Seal)

(Signed) *Mary Walters*_____
Minnesota Notary, Commission Expires 2010
(Official capacity of Officer)

Last Will and Testament

I, _____John Smith_____ a resident of _____Dakota_____ County, Minnesota do hereby make, publish, and declare this to be my Last Will and Testament, hereby revoking any and all Wills and Codicils heretofore made by me.

FIRST: I direct that all my valid debts and funeral expenses be paid out of my estate as soon after my death as is practicable.

SECOND: I make the following special gifts:

If I have made one of more written lists which have been signed by me, and dated, and otherwise prepared in accordance with the Minnesota law M.S.A. Section 524.2-513, then I give the property described in such list or lists to the person or persons named in such list(s) who survive me. I give all tangible personal property not effectively distributed by the provisions of any such written list to: _____

THIRD: I give, devise, and bequeath all my estate, real, personal, and mixed, of whatever kind and wherever situated, of which I may die seized or possessed, or in which I may have any interest or over which I may have any power of appointment or testamentary disposition, to my spouse, _____Barbara Smith_____. If my said spouse does not survive me, I give, and bequeath the said property to my children _____Amy Smith, Beamy Smith, and_____ _____Seamy Smith----------_____ _____, in equal shares or to their lineal descendants, per stirpes.

FOURTH: In the event that any beneficiary fails to survive me by thirty days, then this will shall take effect as if that person had predeceased me.

FIFTH: I hereby nominate, constitute, and appoint _____Barbara Smith_____ as Personal Representative of this, my Last Will and Testament. In the event that such named person is unable or unwilling to serve at any time or for any reason, then I nominate, constitute, and appoint _____Reginald Smith_____ as Personal Representative in the place and stead of the person first named herein. It is my will and I direct that my Personal Representative shall not be required to furnish a bond for the faithful performance of his or her duties in any jurisdiction, any provision of law to the contrary notwithstanding, and I give my Personal Representative full power to administer my estate, including the power to settle claims, pay debts, and sell, lease or exchange real and personal property without court order.

I, _____John Smith_____ the testator, sign my name to this instrument this __29th__ day of __January 2002__, and being first duly sworn, do hereby declare to the undersigned authority that I sign and execute this instrument as my will and that
1) I sign it willingly
    or

Page ___ of ___

2) IF RELEVANT TO YOUR SITUATION: I willingly direct another to sign for me,

and that I execute it as my free and voluntary act for the purposes therein expressed, and that I am 18 years of age or older, of sound mind, and under no constraint or undue influence.

John Smith
_____
Testator

We, _Betty Brown, John Doe_, the witnesses, sign our names to this instrument, being first duly sworn, and do hereby declare to the undersigned authority that the testator signs and executes this instrument as the testator's will and that the testator

1) signs it willingly
    or
2) IF RELEVANT TO YOUR SITUATION: willingly directs another to sign for the testator

and that each of us, in the presence and hearing of the testator, hereby signs this will as witness to the testator's signing, and that to the best of our knowledge the testator is 18 years of age or older, of sound mind, and under no constraint or undue influence.

Betty Brown
_____
Witness

John Doe
_____
Witness

State of _Minnesota_
County of _Dakota_

Subscribed, sworn to, and acknowledged before me by _John Smith_, the testator, and subscribed and sworn to before me by ___Betty Brown___, and _John Doe_, Witnesses, this _29th_ day of _January 2002_
(Notary Seal)

(Signed) _____*Tod Yang*_____
  Minnesota Notary, Commission Expires 2010
  (Official capacity of Officer)

Last Will and Testament

I, _____John Doe_____ a resident of _____St. Louis_____
County, Minnesota do hereby make, publish, and declare this to be my Last Will and Testament, hereby revoking any and all Wills and Codicils heretofore made by me.

FIRST: I direct that all my just debts and funeral expenses be paid out of my estate as soon after my death as is practicable.

SECOND: I make the following special gifts:

If I have made one of more written lists which have been signed by me, and dated, and otherwise prepared in accordance with the Minnesota law M.S.A. Section 524.2-513, then I give the property described in such list or lists to the person or persons named in such list(s) who survive me. I give all tangible personal property not effectively distributed by the provisions of any such written list to: _____

THIRD: I give, devise, and bequeath all my estate, real, personal, and mixed, of whatever kind and wherever situated, of which I may die seized or possessed, or in which I may have any interest or over which I may have any power of appointment or testamentary disposition, to my children James Doe, Mary Doe, Larry Doe, Barry Doe, Carrie Doe, and Moe Doe ----
_____
_____,
plus any afterborn or adopted children in equal shares or to their lineal descendants per stirpes.

FOURTH: In the event that any beneficiary fails to survive me by thirty days, then this will shall take effect as if that person had predeceased me.

FIFTH: In the event any of my children have not attained the age of 18 years at the time of my death, I hereby nominate, constitute, and appoint _____Herbert Doe_____
as guardian over the person of any of my children who have not reached the age of majority at the time of my death. In the event that said guardian is unable or unwilling to serve, then I nominate, constitute, and appoint _____Tom Doe_____ as guardian. Said guardian shall serve without bond or surety.

SIXTH: In the event any of my children have not attained the age of 18 years at the time of my death, I hereby nominate, constitute, and appoint _____Herbert Doe_____
as guardian over the property of any of my children who have not reached the age of majority at the time of my death. In the event that said guardian is unable or unwilling to serve, then I nominate, constitute, and appoint _____Tom Doe_____ as guardian. Said guardian shall serve without bond or surety.

SEVENTII: I hereby nominate, constitute, and appoint _____Clarence Doe_____ as Personal Representative of this, my Last Will and Testament. In the event that such named person is unable or unwilling to serve at any time or for any reason, then I nominate, constitute, and appoint
Page ____ of ____

_____Englebert Doe_____ as Personal Representative in the place and stead of the person first named herein. It is my will and I direct that my Personal Representative shall not be required to furnish a bond for the faithful performance of his or her duties in any jurisdiction, any provision of law to the contrary notwithstanding, and I give my Personal Representative full power to administer my estate, including the power to settle claims, pay debts, and sell, lease or exchange real and personal property without court order.

     I, _John Doe_____ the testator, sign my name to this instrument this _2nd_ day of _July 2002_____ and being first duly sworn, do hereby declare to the undersigned authority that I sign and execute this instrument as my will and that

1) I sign it willingly

or

2) IF RELEVANT TO YOUR SITUATION: I willingly direct another to sign for me,

and that I execute it as my free and voluntary act for the purposes therein expressed, and that I am 18 years of age or older, of sound mind, and under no constraint or undue influence.

*John Doe*_____
Testator

We, _Mary Jones, John Smith_____, the witnesses, sign our names to this instrument, being first duly sworn, and do hereby declare to the undersigned authority that the testator signs and executes this instrument as the testator's will and that the testator

1) signs it willingly

or

2) IF RELEVANT TO YOUR SITUATION: willingly directs another to sign for the testator,

and that each of us, in the presence and hearing of the testator, hereby signs this will as witness to the testator's signing, and that to the best of our knowledge the testator is 18 years of age or older, of sound mind, and under no constraint or undue influence.

*Mary Jones*_____
Witness

*John Smith*_____
Witness

State of _Minnesota_____
County of _St. Louis___

Subscribed, sworn to, and acknowledged before me by _John Doe_, the testator, and subscribed and sworn to before me by _Mary Jones and John Smith_ Witnesses, this _29th_ day of _July 2002_____.
(Notary Seal)
(Signed) _____*Stoney LaRoc*_____
  Minnesota Notary, Commission Expires 2010
  (Official capacity of Officer)

Page ___ of ___

Last Will and Testament

I, _____Mary Smith_____ a resident of _Ramsey_____
County, Minnesota do hereby make, publish, and declare this to be my Last Will and Testament, hereby revoking any and all Wills and Codicils heretofore made by me.

FIRST: I direct that all my just debts and funeral expenses be paid out of my estate as soon after my death as is practicable.

SECOND: I make the following special gifts:

If I have made one of more written lists which have been signed by me, and dated, and otherwise prepared in accordance with the Minnesota law M.S.A. Section 524.2-513, then I give the property described in such list or lists to the person or persons named in such list(s) who survive me. I give all tangible personal property not effectively distributed by the provisions of any such written list to: _____

THIRD: I give, devise, and bequeath all my estate, real, personal, and mixed, of whatever kind and wherever situated, of which I may die seized or possessed, or in which I may have any interest or over which I may have any power of appointment or testamentary disposition, to the following:_ my brothers John Smith and James Smith ------------------------
_____
_____,
or to the survivor of them.

FOURTH: In the event that any beneficiary fails to survive me by thirty days, then this will shall take effect as if that person had predeceased me.

FIFTH: I hereby nominate, constitute, and appoint _Herbert Doe_____ as Personal Representative of this, my Last Will and Testament. In the event that such named person is unable or unwilling to serve at any time or for any reason, then I nominate, constitute, and appoint _____Tom Doe_____ as Personal Representative in the place and stead of the person first named herein. It is my will and I direct that my Personal Representative shall not be required to furnish a bond for the faithful performance of his or her duties in any jurisdiction, any provision of law to the contrary notwithstanding, and I give my Personal Representative full power to administer my estate, including the power to settle claims, pay debts, and sell, lease or exchange real and personal property without court order.

I, _Mary Smith_ the testator, sign my name to this instrument this _6th_ day of _May 2002_, and being first duly sworn, do hereby declare to the undersigned authority that I sign and execute this instrument as my will and that

1) I sign it willingly
or

Page ___ of ___

2) IF RELEVANT TO YOUR SITUATION: I willingly direct another to sign for me,

and that I execute it as my free and voluntary act for the purposes therein expressed, and that I am 18 years of age or older, of sound mind, and under no constraint or undue influence.

Mary Smith
_____
Testator

We, <u>Leon Brown, Mildred Brown</u>, the witnesses, sign our names to this instrument, being first duly sworn, and do hereby declare to the undersigned authority that the testator signs and executes this instrument as the testator's will and that the testator

1) signs it willingly

or

2) IF RELEVANT TO YOUR SITUATION: willingly directs another to sign for the testator,

and that each of us, in the presence and hearing of the testator, hereby signs this will as witness to the testator's signing, and that to the best of our knowledge the testator is 18 years of age or older, of sound mind, and under no constraint or undue influence.

Leon Brown
_____
Witness

Mildred Brown
_____
Witness

State of <u>Minnesota</u>
County of <u>Ramsey</u>

Subscribed, sworn to, and acknowledged before me by John Smith, the testator, and subscribed and sworn to before me by <u>Leon Brown</u>, and <u>Mildred Brown</u>, Witnesses, this <u>29th</u> day of <u>January 2002</u>.

(Notary Seal)
(Signed) _____*Donna Black*_____

Minnesota Notary, Commission Expires 2010
(Official capacity of Officer)

Page ___ of ___

Self-Proved Will Affidavit

(attach to Will)

STATE OF Minnesota

COUNTY OF Hennepin

      We, <u>John Doe, Jane Roe, and Melvin Coe</u> the testator and witnesses, respectively, whose names are signed to the attached or foregoing instrument, being first duly sworn, do hereby declare to the undersigned authority that the testator signed and executed the instrument as the testator's will and that the testator

1) signed willingly

or

2) IF RELEVANT TO YOUR SITUATION willingly directed another to sign for the testator

and that the testator executed it as the testator's free and voluntary act for the

purposes therein expressed, and each of the witnesses, in the presence and hearing of the testator, signed the will as witness and that to the best of the witness' knowledge the testator was at the time 18 years of age or older, of sound mind, and under no constraint or undue influence.

John Doe
_____
Testator

Jane Roe
_____
Witness

Melvin Coe
_____
Witness

Subscribed, sworn to, and acknowledged before me by <u>John Doe</u>, the testator, and subscribed and sworn to before me by <u>Jane Roe and Melvin Coe</u> Witnesses, this <u>5th</u> day of <u>July 2002</u>.

(Notary Seal)

(Signed)_<u>*C.U. Sine*</u>_____

      Notary or Other Officer, Commission expires 2010

      (Official capacity of Officer)

Page ___ of ___

Codicil to the Will of

_____ Larry Lowe _____

I, _____ Larry Lowe _____, a resident of _____ Lake _____
County, Minnesota declare this to be the first codicil to my Last Will and Testament dated
_____ July 5 _____, __ 2003__.

FIRST: I hereby revoke the clause of my Will which reads as follows:
__FOURTH: I hereby leave $5000.00 to my daughter Mildred_____
_____
_____
_____.

SECOND: I hereby add the following clause to my Will: _____
__FOURTH: I hereby leave $1000.00 to my daughter Mildred_____
_____
_____
_____.

THIRD: In all other respects I hereby confirm and republish my Last Will and Testament
dated _____ July 5 _____, __ 2003__ .

STATE OF Minnesota
COUNTY OF Lake

We, __Larry Lowe, Mary Smith, and James Smith__ testator and the witnesses, respectively, whose names are signed to the attached or foregoing instrument, being first duly sworn, do hereby declare to the undersigned authority that the testator signed and executed the foregoing instrument as a codicil to the testator's will; and that the testator

1) had signed willingly
or
2) IF RELEVANT TO YOUR SITUATION: willingly directed another to sign for the testator,

and that the testator executed it as the testator's free and voluntary act for the purposes therein expressed, and each of the witnesses, in the presence and hearing of the testator, signed the will as witness and that to the best of the witness' knowledge the testator was at the time 18 years of age or older, of sound mind, and under no constraint or undue influence.

Page ___ of ___

Larry Lowe
_____
Testator

Mary Smith
_____
Witness

James Smith
_____
Witness

Subscribed, sworn to, and acknowledged before me by <u>Larry Lowe</u>, the testator, and subscribed and sworn to before me by <u>Mary Smith and James Smith</u>, Witnesses, this <u>5th</u> day of <u>July 2005</u>.

(Notary Seal)

(Signed) **_I.C. Usighne_**
_____

        Minnesota Notary, Commission expires 2010
        (Official capacity of Officer)

Page ___ of ___

Appendix C
Blank Forms

The following pages contain forms that can be used to prepare a will, codicil, living will, and Anatomical (Organ) Donation. They should only be used by persons who have read this book completely, who do not have any complications in their legal affairs, and who understand the forms they are using. The forms may be used right out of the book or they may be photocopied or retyped.

You may need legal or financial advice to prepare these forms if they do not meet your particular situation or if questions about the law remain after you read the book.

How to Pick the Right Will

Follow the chart and use the form number in the black circle,
then use form 17, the self-proving affidavit

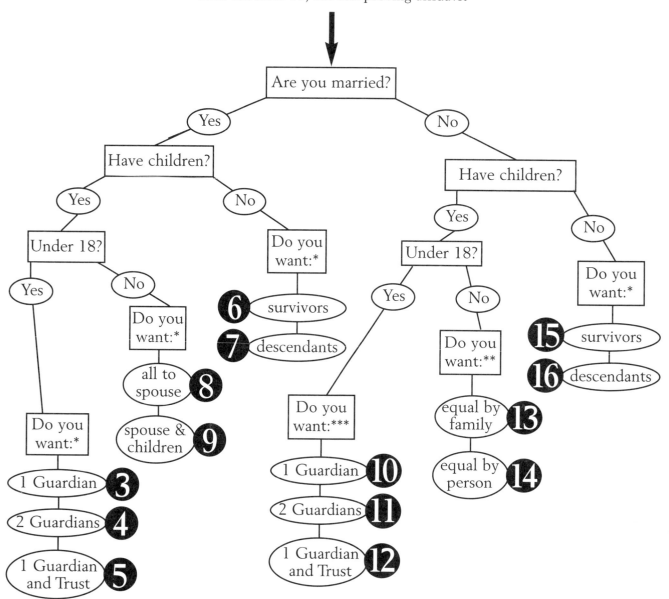

2 Be sure to use form 2, the **GIFTS, PREFERENCES AND INFORMATION LIST**. The special gifts list, if you use it, must be mentioned in your will. Some special gifts can be listed in your will, but every time you change them, you have to make a new will or codicil.

17 Be sure to use form 17, the **SELF-PROVING AFFIDAVIT** with your will, no matter which form you use.

* For an explanation of survivors/descendants, see page ___.
** For an explanation of families/persons, see page ___.
*** For an explanation of children's guardians and trust, see page ___.

Asset and Beneficiary List

Property Inventory

Assets

Bank Accounts (checking, savings, certificates of deposit, coin collections)

_____
_____
_____
_____
_____
_____
_____

Real Estate (include ice fishing houses)

_____
_____
_____
_____
_____
_____
_____

Vehicles (cars, trucks, boats, snowmobiles, motorcycles, planes, RVs, etc.) (List name(s) on each title)

_____
_____
_____
_____
_____
_____
_____

Personal Property (collections, jewelry, tools, artwork, household items, etc.) (Attach appraisals)

_____
_____
_____
_____
_____
_____
_____

_____
_____
_____
_____
_____
_____
_____

Stocks/Bonds/Mutual Funds

_____
_____
_____
_____
_____
_____
_____
_____
_____
_____
_____
_____
_____

Retirement Accounts (IRAs, 401(k)s, pension plans, etc.)

_____
_____
_____
_____
_____
_____
_____

Receivables (mortgages held, notes, accounts receivable, personal loans)

_____
_____
_____
_____
_____
_____
_____

Life Insurance

_____
_____
_____
_____
_____
_____
_____

Other Property (trusts, partnerships, businesses, profit sharing, copyrights, etc.)

_____
_____
_____
_____
_____
_____
_____

Liabilities

Real Estate Loans

_____
_____
_____
_____
_____
_____
_____

Vehicle Loans

_____
_____
_____
_____
_____
_____
_____

Other Secured Loans

_____
_____
_____
_____
_____
_____
_____

Unsecured Loans and Debts (taxes, child support, judgments, etc.)

_____
_____
_____
_____
_____
_____
_____

Beneficiary List

Name_____ Address_____ Phone_____
_____

Name_____ Address_____ Phone_____
_____

Name_____ Address_____ Phone_____
_____

Name_____ Address_____ Phone_____
_____

Name_____ Address_____ Phone_____
_____

Special Gifts, Preferences and Information List

Statement of Desires, Location of Property & Documents, and List of Personal Property with Names of Each Person Who Will Receive Each Item

I, _____, am signing this document as the expression of my desires as to the matters stated below, and to inform my family members or other significant persons of the location of certain property and documents in the event of any emergency or of my death.

1.   **Funeral Desires.** It is my desire that the following arrangements be made for my funeral and disposition of remains in the event of my death (state if you have made any arrangements, such as pre-paid burial plans, cemetery plots owned, etc.). These arrangements may <u>also</u> be listed in your organ donation declaration.

       Burial at _____
_____.

       Cremation at _____
_____.

       Other specific desires: _____
_____
_____.

2.   **Pets.** I have the following pet(s): _____
_____. The following are my desires concerning the
care of said pet(s): _____
_____
_____.

4.   **Notification.** I would like the following person(s) notified in the event of emergency or death (give name, address and phone number):

_____
_____
_____
_____
_____.

5.   **Location of Documents.** The following is a list of important documents, and their location:

       Last Will and Testament, dated _____. Location: _____
_____.

       Advance Health Care Directive, dated _____. Location: _____
_____.

       Deed(s) to real estate (describe property location, including the state; location of deed); list all names on the title

_____
_____
_____

       Honorable Discharge Papers

Title(s) to vehicles (cars, boats, etc.) (Describe each vehicle, its location, and location of title, registration, or other documents):

_____

_____

_____

_____

Life insurance policies (list name address & phone number of insurance company and insurance agent, policy number, and location of policy; list beneficiaries: names, addresses, and phone numbers; insurance companies do not contact beneficiaries when you die):

_____

_____

_____

Other insurance policies (list type, company & agent, policy number, and location of policy):

_____

_____

_____

Other: (list other documents such as stock certificates, bonds, certificates of deposit, mutual funds, brokerage accounts, IRAs, pension plans, and all other retirement accounts, and the location of each):

_____

_____

_____

6. **Location of Assets.** In addition to items readily visible in my home or listed above, I have the following assets:

Safe deposit box located at _____, box number _____. Key located at: _____.

Bank accounts (list name & address of bank, type of account, and account number):

_____

Other (describe the item and give its location):

_____

_____

_____

_____

_____

7. Other desires or information (state any desires or provide any information not given above; use additional sheets of paper if necessary):

_____

_____

_____

_____

_____

8. List each item of personal tangible property and the full name of the person who is to receive it. Existence of this list must be mentioned in your will. Original should be kept with the will.

_____

_____

_____

Dated: _____

_____

Signature

Last Will and Testament

I, _____ a resident of _____ County, Minnesota do hereby make, publish, and declare this to be my Last Will and Testament, hereby revoking any and all Wills and Codicils heretofore made by me.

FIRST: I direct that all my valid debts and funeral expenses be paid out of my estate as soon after my death as is practicable.

SECOND: I make the following special gifts:

If I have made one of more written lists which have been signed by me, and dated, and otherwise prepared in accordance with the Minnesota law M.S.A. Section 524.2-513, then I give the property described in such list or lists to the person or persons named in such list(s) who survive me. I give all tangible personal property not effectively distributed by the provisions of any such written list to: _____

THIRD: I give, devise, and bequeath all my estate, real, personal, and mixed, of whatever kind and wherever situated, of which I may die seized or possessed, or in which I may have any interest or over which I may have any power of appointment or testamentary disposition, to my spouse, _____. If my said spouse does not survive me, I give, and bequeath the said property to my children _____
_____
_____,
plus any afterborn or adopted children in equal shares or their lineal descendants, per stirpes.

FOURTH: In the event that any beneficiary fails to survive me by thirty days, then this will shall take effect as if that person had predeceased me.

FIFTH: Should my spouse not survive me, I hereby nominate, constitute, and appoint _____ as guardian over the person and estate of any of my children who have not reached the age of majority at the time of my death. In the event that said guardian is unable or unwilling to serve, then I nominate, constitute, and appoint _____ as guardian. Said guardian shall serve without bond or surety.

SIXTH: I hereby nominate, constitute, and appoint _____ as Personal Representative of this, my Last Will and Testament. In the event that such named person is unable or unwilling to serve at any time or for any reason, then I nominate, constitute, and appoint _____ as Personal Representative in the place and stead of the person first named herein. It is my will and I direct that my Personal Representative shall not be required to furnish a bond for the faithful performance of his or her duties in any jurisdiction, any provision of law to the contrary notwithstanding, and I give my Personal Representative full power to administer my estate, including the power to settle claims, pay debts, and sell, lease or exchange real and personal property without court order.

Page ___ of ___

I, _____ the testator, sign my name to this instrument this _____ day of _____, and being first duly sworn, do hereby declare to the undersigned authority that I sign and execute this instrument as my will and that

1) I sign it willingly

    or

2) IF RELEVANT TO YOUR SITUATION: I willingly direct another to sign for me,

and that I execute it as my free and voluntary act for the purposes therein expressed, and that I am 18 years of age or older, of sound mind, and under no constraint or undue influence.

_____

Testator

We, _____, the witnesses, sign our names to this instrument, being first duly sworn, and do hereby declare to the undersigned authority that the testator signs and executes this instrument as the testator's will and that the testator

1) signs it willingly

or

2) IF RELEVANT TO YOUR SITUATION: willingly directs another to sign for the testator

and that each of us, in the presence and hearing of the testator, hereby signs this will as witness to the testator's signing, and that to the best of our knowledge the testator is 18 years of age or older, of sound mind, and under no constraint or undue influence.

_____

Witness

_____

Witness

State of _____

County of _____

Subscribed, sworn to, and acknowledged before me by _____, the testator, and subscribed and sworn to before me by _____, and _____ Witnesses, this _____ day of _____, _____.
(Notary Seal)
(Signed) _____
   Minnesota Notary, Commission Expires: _____
   (Official capacity of Officer)

Last Will and Testament

I, _____ a resident of _____ County, Minnesota do hereby make, publish, and declare this to be my Last Will and Testament, hereby revoking any and all Wills and Codicils heretofore made by me.

FIRST: I direct that all my valid debts and funeral expenses be paid out of my estate as soon after my death as is practicable.

SECOND: I make the following special gifts:

If I have made one of more written lists which have been signed by me, and dated, and otherwise prepared in accordance with the Minnesota law M.S.A. Section 524.2-513, then I give the property described in such list or lists to the person or persons named in such list(s) who survive me. I give all tangible personal property not effectively distributed by the provisions of any such written list to: _____

THIRD: I give, devise, and bequeath all my estate, real, personal, and mixed, of whatever kind and wherever situated, of which I may die seized or possessed, or in which I may have any interest or over which I may have any power of appointment or testamentary disposition, to my spouse, _____. If my said spouse does not survive me, I give, and bequeath the said property to my children _____ _____ _____, plus any afterborn or adopted children in equal shares or their lineal descendants, per stirpes.

FOURTH: In the event that any beneficiary fails to survive me by thirty days, then this will shall take effect as if that person had predeceased me.

FIFTH: Should my spouse not survive me, I hereby nominate, constitute, and appoint _____, as guardian over the person of any of my children who have not reached the age of majority at the time of my death. In the event that said guardian is unable or unwilling to serve, then I nominate, constitute, and appoint _____ as guardian. Said guardian shall serve without bond or surety.

SIXTH: Should my spouse not survive me, I hereby nominate, constitute, and appoint _____ as guardian over the estate of any of my children who have not reached the age of majority at the time of my death. In the event that said guardian is unable or unwilling to serve, then I nominate, constitute, and appoint _____ as guardian. Said guardian shall serve without bond or surety.

SEVENTH: I hereby nominate, constitute, and appoint _____ as Personal Representative of this, my Last Will and Testament. In the event that such named person is unable or unwilling to serve at any time or for any reason, then I nominate, constitute, and appoint _____ as Personal Representative in the place and stead of the person first named herein. It is my will and I direct that my Personal Representative shall not be

Page ___ of ___

required to furnish a bond for the faithful performance of his or her duties in any jurisdiction, any provision of law to the contrary notwithstanding, and I give my Personal Representative full power to administer my estate, including the power to settle claims, pay debts, and sell, lease or exchange real and personal property without court order.

I, _____ the testator, sign my name to this instrument this _____ day of _____, and being first duly sworn, do hereby declare to the undersigned authority that I sign and execute this instrument as my will and that

1) I sign it willingly
      or
2)   IF RELEVANT TO YOUR SITUATION: I willingly direct another to sign for me,

and that I execute it as my free and voluntary act for the purposes therein expressed, and that I am 18 years of age or older, of sound mind, and under no constraint or undue influence.

_____
Testator

We, _____, the witnesses, sign our names to this instrument, being first duly sworn, and do hereby declare to the undersigned authority that the testator signs and executes this instrument as the testator's will and that the testator

1) signs it willingly
or
2) IF RELEVANT TO YOUR SITUATION: willingly directs another to sign for the testator

and that each of us, in the presence and hearing of the testator, hereby signs this will as witness to the testator's signing, and that to the best of our knowledge the testator is 18 years of age or older, of sound mind, and under no constraint or undue influence.

_____
Witness

_____
Witness

State of _____
County of _____

Subscribed, sworn to, and acknowledged before me by _____, the testator, and subscribed and sworn to before me by _____, and _____ Witnesses, this _____ day of _____, _____.
(Notary Seal)
(Signed) _____
   Minnesota Notary, Commission Expires: _____
   (Official capacity of Officer)

Page ___ of ___

Last Will and Testament

I, _____ a resident of _____ County, Minnesota do hereby make, publish, and declare this to be my Last Will and Testament, hereby revoking any and all Wills and Codicils heretofore made by me.

FIRST: I direct that all my valid debts and funeral expenses be paid out of my estate as soon after my death as is practicable.

SECOND: I make the following special gifts:

If I have made one of more written lists which have been signed by me, and dated, and otherwise prepared in accordance with the Minnesota law M.S.A. Section 524.2-513, then I give the property described in such list or lists to the person or persons named in such list(s) who survive me. I give all tangible personal property not effectively distributed by the provisions of any such written list to: _____

THIRD: I give, devise, and bequeath all my estate, real, personal, and mixed, of whatever kind and wherever situated, of which I may die seized or possessed, or in which I may have any interest or over which I may have any power of appointment or testamentary disposition, to my spouse, _____. If my said spouse does not survive me, I give, and bequeath the said property to my children _____ _____ _____, plus any afterborn or adopted children in equal shares or their lineal descendants, per stirpes.

FOURTH: In the event that any beneficiary fails to survive me by thirty days, then this will shall take effect as if that person had predeceased me.

FIFTH: In the event that any of my children have not reached the age of _____ years at the time of my death, then the share of any such child shall be held in a separate trust by _____ for such child.

The trustee shall use the income and that part of the principal of the trust as is, in the trustee's sole discretion, necessary or desirable to provide proper housing, medical care, food, clothing, entertainment and education for the trust beneficiary, considering the beneficiary's other resources. Any income that is not distributed shall be added to the principal. Additionally, the trustee shall have all powers conferred by the law of the state having jurisdiction over this trust, as well as the power to pay from the assets of the trust reasonable fees necessary to administer the trust.

The trust shall terminate when the child reaches the age specified above and the remaining assets distributed to the child, unless they have been exhausted sooner. In the event the child dies prior to the termination of the trust, then the assets shall pass to the estate of the child. The interests of the beneficiary under this trust shall not be assignable and shall be free from the claims of creditors to the full extent allowed by law.

In the event the said trustee is unable or unwilling to serve for any reason, then I nominate, constitute, and appoint _____ as alternate trustee. No bond

Page ___ of ___

shall be required of either trustee in any jurisdiction and this trust shall be administered without court supervision as allowed by law.

SIXTH: Should my spouse not survive me, I hereby nominate, constitute, and appoint _____as guardian over the person and estate of any of my children who have not reached the age of majority at the time of my death. In the event that said guardian is unable or unwilling to serve, then I nominate, constitute, and appoint _____ as guardian.

SEVENTH: I hereby nominate, constitute, and appoint _____ as Personal Representative of this, my Last Will and Testament. In the event that such named person is unable or unwilling to serve at any time or for any reason, then I nominate, constitute, and appoint _____ as Personal Representative in the place and stead of the person first named herein. It is my will and I direct that my Personal Representative shall not be required to furnish a bond for the faithful performance of his or her duties in any jurisdiction, any provision of law to the contrary notwithstanding, and I give my Personal Representative full power to administer my estate, including the power to settle claims, pay debts, and sell, lease or exchange real and personal property without court order.

I, _____ the testator, sign my name to this instrument this _____ day of _____, and being first duly sworn, do hereby declare to the undersigned authority that I sign and execute this instrument as my will and that

1) I sign it willingly

    or

2) IF RELEVANT TO YOUR SITUATION: I willingly direct another to sign for me,

and that I execute it as my free and voluntary act for the purposes therein expressed, and that I am 18 years of age or older, of sound mind, and under no constraint or undue influence.

_____
Testator

We, _____, the witnesses, sign our names to this instrument, being first duly sworn, and do hereby declare to the undersigned authority that the testator signs and executes this instrument as the testator's will and that the testator

1) signs it willingly

or

2) IF RELEVANT TO YOUR SITUATION: willingly directs another to sign for the testator

and that each of us, in the presence and hearing of the testator, hereby signs this will as witness to the testator's signing, and that to the best of our knowledge the testator is 18 years of age or older, of sound mind, and under no constraint or undue influence.

_____
Witness
_____
Witness

State of _____
County of _____

Subscribed, sworn to, and acknowledged before me by ____ _____, the testator, and subscribed and sworn to before me by _____, and _____ Witnesses, this _____ day of _____, _____.
(Notary Seal)
(Signed) _____
  Minnesota Notary, Commission Expires: _____
  (Official capacity of Officer)

Last Will and Testament

I, _____ a resident of _____
County, Minnesota do hereby make, publish, and declare this to be my Last Will and Testament, hereby revoking any and all Wills and Codicils heretofore made by me.

FIRST: I direct that all my valid debts and funeral expenses be paid out of my estate as soon after my death as is practicable.

SECOND: I make the following special gifts:

If I have made one of more written lists which have been signed by me, and dated, and otherwise prepared in accordance with the Minnesota law M.S.A. Section 524.2-513, then I give the property described in such list or lists to the person or persons named in such list(s) who survive me. I give all tangible personal property not effectively distributed by the provisions of any such written list to: _____

THIRD: I give, devise, and bequeath all my estate, real, personal, and mixed, of whatever kind and wherever situated, of which I may die seized or possessed, or in which I may have any interest or over which I may have any power of appointment or testamentary disposition, to my spouse, _____. If my said spouse does not survive me, I give, and bequeath the said property to _____
_____
_____ ,
or the survivor of them.

FOURTH: In the event that any beneficiary fails to survive me by thirty days, then this will shall take effect as if that person had predeceased me.

FIFTH: I hereby nominate, constitute, and appoint _____ as Personal Representative of this, my Last Will and Testament. In the event that such named person is unable or unwilling to serve at any time or for any reason, then I nominate, constitute, and appoint _____ as Personal Representative in the place and stead of the person first named herein. It is my will and I direct that my Personal Representative shall not be required to furnish a bond for the faithful performance of his or her duties in any jurisdiction, any provision of law to the contrary notwithstanding, and I give my Personal Representative full power to administer my estate, including the power to settle claims, pay debts, and sell, lease or exchange real and personal property without court order.

I, _____ the testator, sign my name to this instrument this _____ day of _____, and being first duly sworn, do hereby declare to the undersigned authority that I sign and execute this instrument as my will and that

1) I sign it willingly
      or

2) IF RELEVANT TO YOUR SITUATION: I willingly direct another to sign for me,

and that I execute it as my free and voluntary act for the purposes therein expressed, and that I am 18 years of age or older, of sound mind, and under no constraint or undue influence.

_____
Testator

We, _____, the witnesses, sign our names to this instrument, being first duly sworn, and do hereby declare to the undersigned authority that the testator signs and executes this instrument as the testator's will and that the testator

1) signs it willingly

or

2) IF RELEVANT TO YOUR SITUATION: willingly directs another to sign for the testator

and that each of us, in the presence and hearing of the testator, hereby signs this will as witness to the testator's signing, and that to the best of our knowledge the testator is 18 years of age or older, of sound mind, and under no constraint or undue influence.

_____
Witness

_____
Witness

State of _____
County of _____

Subscribed, sworn to, and acknowledged before me by _____, the testator, and subscribed and sworn to before me by _____, and _____ Witnesses, this _____ day of _____, _____.
(Notary Seal)
(Signed) _____
   Minnesota Notary, Commission Expires: _____
   (Official capacity of Officer)

Last Will and Testament

I, _____ a resident of _____ County, Minnesota do hereby make, publish, and declare this to be my Last Will and Testament, hereby revoking any and all Wills and Codicils heretofore made by me.

FIRST: I direct that all my valid debts and funeral expenses be paid out of my estate as soon after my death as is practicable.

SECOND: I make the following special gifts:

If I have made one of more written lists which have been signed by me, and dated, and otherwise prepared in accordance with the Minnesota law M.S.A. Section 524.2-513, then I give the property described in such list or lists to the person or persons named in such list(s) who survive me. I give all tangible personal property not effectively distributed by the provisions of any such written list to: _____

THIRD: I give, devise, and bequeath all my estate, real, personal, and mixed, of whatever kind and wherever situated, of which I may die seized or possessed, or in which I may have any interest or over which I may have any power of appointment or testamentary disposition, to my spouse, _____. If my said spouse does not survive me, I give, and bequeath the said property to _____ _____ _____, or to their lineal descendants, per stirpes.

FOURTH: In the event that any beneficiary fails to survive me by thirty days, then this will shall take effect as if that person had predeceased me.

FIFTH: I hereby nominate, constitute, and appoint _____ as Personal Representative of this, my Last Will and Testament. In the event that such named person is unable or unwilling to serve at any time or for any reason, then I nominate, constitute, and appoint _____ as Personal Representative in the place and stead of the person first named herein. It is my will and I direct that my Personal Representative shall not be required to furnish a bond for the faithful performance of his or her duties in any jurisdiction, any provision of law to the contrary notwithstanding, and I give my Personal Representative full power to administer my estate, including the power to settle claims, pay debts, and sell, lease or exchange real and personal property without court order.

I, _____ the testator, sign my name to this instrument this _____ day of _____, and being first duly sworn, do hereby declare to the undersigned authority that I sign and execute this instrument as my will and that

1) I sign it willingly
    or

2) IF RELEVANT TO YOUR SITUATION: I willingly direct another to sign for me,

and that I execute it as my free and voluntary act for the purposes therein expressed, and that I am 18 years of age or older, of sound mind, and under no constraint or undue influence.

_____

Testator

We, _____, the witnesses, sign our names to this instrument, being first duly sworn, and do hereby declare to the undersigned authority that the testator signs and executes this instrument as the testator's will and that the testator

1) signs it willingly

or

2) IF RELEVANT TO YOUR SITUATION: willingly directs another to sign for the testator

and that each of us, in the presence and hearing of the testator, hereby signs this will as witness to the testator's signing, and that to the best of our knowledge the testator is 18 years of age or older, of sound mind, and under no constraint or undue influence.

_____

Witness

_____

Witness

State of _____
County of _____

Subscribed, sworn to, and acknowledged before me by _____, the testator, and subscribed and sworn to before me by _____, and _____ Witnesses, this _____ day of _____, _____.
(Notary Seal)
(Signed) _____
   Minnesota Notary, Commission Expires: _____
   (Official capacity of Officer)

Page ___ of ___

Last Will and Testament

I, _____ a resident of _____ County, Minnesota do hereby make, publish, and declare this to be my Last Will and Testament, hereby revoking any and all Wills and Codicils heretofore made by me.

FIRST: I direct that all my valid debts and funeral expenses be paid out of my estate as soon after my death as is practicable.

SECOND: I make the following special gifts:

If I have made one of more written lists which have been signed by me, and dated, and otherwise prepared in accordance with the Minnesota law M.S.A. Section 524.2-513, then I give the property described in such list or lists to the person or persons named in such list(s) who survive me. I give all tangible personal property not effectively distributed by the provisions of any such written list to: _____

THIRD: I give, devise, and bequeath all my estate, real, personal, and mixed, of whatever kind and wherever situated, of which I may die seized or possessed, or in which I may have any interest or over which I may have any power of appointment or testamentary disposition, to my spouse, _____. If my said spouse does not survive me, I give, and bequeath the said property to my children _____
_____
_____,
in equal shares or to their lineal descendants, per stirpes.

FOURTH: In the event that any beneficiary fails to survive me by thirty days, then this will shall take effect as if that person had predeceased me.

FIFTH: I hereby nominate, constitute, and appoint _____ as Personal Representative of this, my Last Will and Testament. In the event that such named person is unable or unwilling to serve at any time or for any reason, then I nominate, constitute, and appoint _____ as Personal Representative in the place and stead of the person first named herein. It is my will and I direct that my Personal Representative shall not be required to furnish a bond for the faithful performance of his or her duties in any jurisdiction, any provision of law to the contrary notwithstanding, and I give my Personal Representative full power to administer my estate, including the power to settle claims, pay debts, and sell, lease or exchange real and personal property without court order.

I, _____ the testator, sign my name to this instrument this _____ day of _____, and being first duly sworn, do hereby declare to the undersigned authority that I sign and execute this instrument as my will and that

1) I sign it willingly
    or

2) IF RELEVANT TO YOUR SITUATION: I willingly direct another to sign for me,

and that I execute it as my free and voluntary act for the purposes therein expressed, and that I am 18 years of age or older, of sound mind, and under no constraint or undue influence.

_____
Testator

We, _____, the witnesses, sign our names to this instrument, being first duly sworn, and do hereby declare to the undersigned authority that the testator signs and executes this instrument as the testator's will and that the testator

1) signs it willingly
or
2) IF RELEVANT TO YOUR SITUATION: willingly directs another to sign for the testator

and that each of us, in the presence and hearing of the testator, hereby signs this will as witness to the testator's signing, and that to the best of our knowledge the testator is 18 years of age or older, of sound mind, and under no constraint or undue influence.

_____
Witness

_____
Witness

State of _____
County of _____

Subscribed, sworn to, and acknowledged before me by _____, the testator, and subscribed and sworn to before me by _____, and _____ Witnesses, this _____ day of _____, _____.
(Notary Seal)
(Signed) _____
   Minnesota Notary, Commission Expires: _____
   (Official capacity of Officer)

Page ___ of ___

Last Will and Testament

I, _____ a resident of _____ County, Minnesota do hereby make, publish, and declare this to be my Last Will and Testament, hereby revoking any and all Wills and Codicils heretofore made by me.

FIRST: I direct that all my valid debts and funeral expenses be paid out of my estate as soon after my death as is practicable.

SECOND: I make the following special gifts:

If I have made one of more written lists which have been signed by me, and dated, and otherwise prepared in accordance with the Minnesota law M.S.A. Section 524.2-513, then I give the property described in such list or lists to the person or persons named in such list(s) who survive me. I give all tangible personal property not effectively distributed by the provisions of any such written list to: _____

THIRD: I give, devise, and bequeath all my estate, real, personal, and mixed, of whatever kind and wherever situated, of which I may die seized or possessed, or in which I may have any interest or over which I may have any power of appointment or testamentary disposition, as follows: _____% to my spouse, _____ and _____% to my children, _____
_____
_____,
in equal shares or to their lineal descendants per stirpes.

FOURTH: In the event that any beneficiary fails to survive me by thirty days, then this will shall take effect as if that person had predeceased me.

FIFTH: I hereby nominate, constitute, and appoint _____ as Personal Representative of this, my Last Will and Testament. In the event that such named person is unable or unwilling to serve at any time or for any reason, then I nominate, constitute, and appoint _____ as Personal Representative in the place and stead of the person first named herein. It is my will and I direct that my Personal Representative shall not be required to furnish a bond for the faithful performance of his or her duties in any jurisdiction, any provision of law to the contrary notwithstanding, and I give my Personal Representative full power to administer my estate, including the power to settle claims, pay debts, and sell, lease or exchange real and personal property without court order.

I, _____ the testator, sign my name to this instrument this _____ day of _____, and being first duly sworn, do hereby declare to the undersigned authority that I sign and execute this instrument as my will and that

1) I sign it willingly

   or

Page ___ of ___

91

2) IF RELEVANT TO YOUR SITUATION: I willingly direct another to sign for me,

and that I execute it as my free and voluntary act for the purposes therein expressed, and that I am 18 years of age or older, of sound mind, and under no constraint or undue influence.

_____
Testator

We, _____, the witnesses, sign our names to this instrument, being first duly sworn, and do hereby declare to the undersigned authority that the testator signs and executes this instrument as the testator's will and that the testator

1) signs it willingly
or
2) IF RELEVANT TO YOUR SITUATION: willingly directs another to sign for the testator

and that each of us, in the presence and hearing of the testator, hereby signs this will as witness to the testator's signing, and that to the best of our knowledge the testator is 18 years of age or older, of sound mind, and under no constraint or undue influence.

_____
Witness

_____
Witness

State of _____
County of _____

Subscribed, sworn to, and acknowledged before me by _____, the testator, and subscribed and sworn to before me by _____, and _____ Witnesses, this _____ day of _____, _____.
(Notary Seal)
(Signed) _____
    Minnesota Notary, Commission Expires: _____
    (Official capacity of Officer)

Page ___ of ___

Last Will and Testament

I, _____ a resident of _____ County, Minnesota do hereby make, publish, and declare this to be my Last Will and Testament, hereby revoking any and all Wills and Codicils heretofore made by me.

FIRST: I direct that all my valid debts and funeral expenses be paid out of my estate as soon after my death as is practicable.

SECOND: I make the following special gifts:

If I have made one of more written lists which have been signed by me, and dated, and otherwise prepared in accordance with the Minnesota law M.S.A. Section 524.2-513, then I give the property described in such list or lists to the person or persons named in such list(s) who survive me. I give all tangible personal property not effectively distributed by the provisions of any such written list to: _____

THIRD: I give, devise, and bequeath all my estate, real, personal, and mixed, of whatever kind and wherever situated, of which I may die seized or possessed, or in which I may have any interest or over which I may have any power of appointment or testamentary disposition, to my children _____

_____

_____,

plus any afterborn or adopted children in equal shares or to their lineal descendants per stirpes.

FOURTH: In the event that any beneficiary fails to survive me by thirty days, then this will shall take effect as if that person had predeceased me.

FIFTH: In the event any of my children have not attained the age of 18 years at the time of my death, I hereby nominate, constitute, and appoint _____ as guardian over the person and estate of any of my children who have not reached the age of majority at the time of my death. In the event that said guardian is unable or unwilling to serve, then I nominate, constitute, and appoint _____ as guardian. Said guardian shall serve without bond or surety.

SIXTH: I hereby nominate, constitute, and appoint _____ as Personal Representative of this, my Last Will and Testament. In the event that such named person is unable or unwilling to serve at any time or for any reason, then I nominate, constitute, and appoint _____ as Personal Representative in the place and stead of the person first named herein. It is my will and I direct that my Personal Representative shall not be required to furnish a bond for the faithful performance of his or her duties in any jurisdiction, any provision of law to the contrary notwithstanding, and I give my Personal Representative full power to administer my estate, including the power to settle claims, pay debts, and sell, lease or exchange real and personal property without court order.

Page ___ of ___

93

I, _____ the testator, sign my name to this instrument this _____ day of _____, and being first duly sworn, do hereby declare to the undersigned authority that I sign and execute this instrument as my will and that

1) I sign it willingly
   or
2) IF RELEVANT TO YOUR SITUATION: I willingly direct another to sign for me,

and that I execute it as my free and voluntary act for the purposes therein expressed, and that I am 18 years of age or older, of sound mind, and under no constraint or undue influence.

_____
Testator

We, _____, the witnesses, sign our names to this instrument, being first duly sworn, and do hereby declare to the undersigned authority that the testator signs and executes this instrument as the testator's will and that the testator

1) signs it willingly
or
2) IF RELEVANT TO YOUR SITUATION: willingly directs another to sign for the testator

and that each of us, in the presence and hearing of the testator, hereby signs this will as witness to the testator's signing, and that to the best of our knowledge the testator is 18 years of age or older, of sound mind, and under no constraint or undue influence.

_____
Witness

_____
Witness

State of _____
County of _____

Subscribed, sworn to, and acknowledged before me by _____, the testator, and subscribed and sworn to before me by _____, and _____ Witnesses, this _____ day of _____, _____.
(Notary Seal)
(Signed) _____
    Minnesota Notary, Commission Expires: _____
    (Official capacity of Officer)

Page ___ of ___

Last Will and Testament

I, _____ a resident of _____ County, Minnesota do hereby make, publish, and declare this to be my Last Will and Testament, hereby revoking any and all Wills and Codicils heretofore made by me.

FIRST: I direct that all my valid debts and funeral expenses be paid out of my estate as soon after my death as is practicable.

SECOND: I make the following special gifts:

If I have made one of more written lists which have been signed by me, and dated, and otherwise prepared in accordance with the Minnesota law M.S.A. Section 524.2-513, then I give the property described in such list or lists to the person or persons named in such list(s) who survive me. I give all tangible personal property not effectively distributed by the provisions of any such written list to: _____

THIRD: I give, devise, and bequeath all my estate, real, personal, and mixed, of whatever kind and wherever situated, of which I may die seized or possessed, or in which I may have any interest or over which I may have any power of appointment or testamentary disposition, to my children _____

_____

_____,

plus any afterborn or adopted children in equal shares or to their lineal descendants per stirpes.

FOURTH: In the event that any beneficiary fails to survive me by thirty days, then this will shall take effect as if that person had predeceased me.

FIFTH: In the event any of my children have not attained the age of 18 years at the time of my death, I hereby nominate, constitute, and appoint _____ as guardian over the person of any of my children who have not reached the age of majority at the time of my death. In the event that said guardian is unable or unwilling to serve, then I nominate, constitute, and appoint _____ as guardian. Said guardian shall serve without bond or surety.

SIXTH: In the event any of my children have not attained the age of 18 years at the time of my death, I hereby nominate, constitute, and appoint _____ as guardian over the estate of any of my children who have not reached the age of majority at the time of my death. In the event that said guardian is unable or unwilling to serve, then I nominate, constitute, and appoint _____ as guardian. Said guardian shall serve without bond or surety.

SEVENTH: I hereby nominate, constitute, and appoint _____ as Personal Representative of this, my Last Will and Testament. In the event that such named person is unable or unwilling to serve at any time or for any reason, then I nominate, constitute, and appoint _____ as Personal Representative in the place and stead of the person first named herein. It is my will and I direct that my Personal Representative shall not be required to furnish a bond for the faithful performance of his or her duties in any jurisdiction, any provision of law to the contrary notwithstanding, and I give my Personal Representative full power

Page ___ of ___

95

to administer my estate, including the power to settle claims, pay debts, and sell, lease or exchange real and personal property without court order.

I, _____ the testator, sign my name to this instrument this _____ day of _____, and being first duly sworn, do hereby declare to the undersigned authority that I sign and execute this instrument as my will and that

1) I sign it willingly
    or
2) IF RELEVANT TO YOUR SITUATION: I willingly direct another to sign for me,

and that I execute it as my free and voluntary act for the purposes therein expressed, and that I am 18 years of age or older, of sound mind, and under no constraint or undue influence.

_____
Testator

We, _____, the witnesses, sign our names to this instrument, being first duly sworn, and do hereby declare to the undersigned authority that the testator signs and executes this instrument as the testator's will and that the testator

1) signs it willingly
or
2) IF RELEVANT TO YOUR SITUATION: willingly directs another to sign for the testator

and that each of us, in the presence and hearing of the testator, hereby signs this will as witness to the testator's signing, and that to the best of our knowledge the testator is 18 years of age or older, of sound mind, and under no constraint or undue influence.

_____
Witness

_____
Witness

State of _____
County of _____

Subscribed, sworn to, and acknowledged before me by _____, the testator, and subscribed and sworn to before me by _____, and _____ Witnesses, this _____ day of _____, _____.
(Notary Seal)
(Signed) _____
   Minnesota Notary, Commission Expires: _____
   (Official capacity of Officer)

Page ___ of ___

Last Will and Testament

I, _____ a resident of _____ County, Minnesota do hereby make, publish, and declare this to be my Last Will and Testament, hereby revoking any and all Wills and Codicils heretofore made by me.

FIRST: I direct that all my valid debts and funeral expenses be paid out of my estate as soon after my death as is practicable.

SECOND: I make the following special gifts:

If I have made one of more written lists which have been signed by me, and dated, and otherwise prepared in accordance with the Minnesota law M.S.A. Section 524.2-513, then I give the property described in such list or lists to the person or persons named in such list(s) who survive me. I give all tangible personal property not effectively distributed by the provisions of any such written list to: _____

THIRD: I give, devise, and bequeath all my estate, real, personal, and mixed, of whatever kind and wherever situated, of which I may die seized or possessed, or in which I may have any interest or over which I may have any power of appointment or testamentary disposition, to my children _____

_____

_____,

plus any afterborn or adopted children in equal shares or to their lineal descendants per stirpes.

FOURTH: In the event that any beneficiary fails to survive me by thirty days, then this will shall take effect as if that person had predeceased me.

FIFTH: In the event that any of my children have not reached the age of _____ years at the time of my death, then the share of any such child shall be held in a separate trust by _____ for such child.

The trustee shall use the income and that part of the principal of the trust as is, in the trustee's sole discretion, necessary or desirable to provide proper housing, medical care, food, clothing, entertainment and education for the trust beneficiary, considering the beneficiary's other resources. Any income that is not distributed shall be added to the principal. Additionally, the trustee shall have all powers conferred by the law of the state having jurisdiction over this trust, as well as the power to pay from the assets of the trust reasonable fees necessary to administer the trust.

The trust shall terminate when the child reaches the age specified above and the remaining assets distributed to the child, unless they have been exhausted sooner. In the event the child dies prior to the termination of the trust, then the assets shall pass to the estate of the child. The interests of the beneficiary under this trust shall not be assignable and shall be free from the claims of creditors to the full extent allowed by law.

In the event the said trustee is unable or unwilling to serve for any reason, then I nominate, constitute, and appoint _____ as alternate trustee. No bond shall be required of either trustee in any jurisdiction and this trust shall be administered without court supervision as allowed by law.

SIXTH: In the event any of my children have not attained the age of 18 years at the time of my death, I hereby nominate, constitute, and appoint _____ as guardian over the person and estate of any of my children who have not reached the age of majority at the time of my death. In the event that said guardian is unable or unwilling to serve, then I

Page ___ of ___

nominate, constitute, and appoint _____ as guardian. Said guardian shall serve without bond or surety.

SEVENTH: I hereby nominate, constitute, and appoint _____ as Personal Representative of this, my Last Will and Testament. In the event that such named person is unable or unwilling to serve at any time or for any reason, then I nominate, constitute, and appoint _____ as Personal Representative in the place and stead of the person first named herein. It is my will and I direct that my Personal Representative shall not be required to furnish a bond for the faithful performance of his or her duties in any jurisdiction, any provision of law to the contrary notwithstanding, and I give my Personal Representative full power to administer my estate, including the power to settle claims, pay debts, and sell, lease or exchange real and personal property without court order.

I, _____ the testator, sign my name to this instrument this _____ day of _____, and being first duly sworn, do hereby declare to the undersigned authority that I sign and execute this instrument as my will and that

1) I sign it willingly
    or
2) IF RELEVANT TO YOUR SITUATION: I willingly direct another to sign for me,

and that I execute it as my free and voluntary act for the purposes therein expressed, and that I am 18 years of age or older, of sound mind, and under no constraint or undue influence.

_____
Testator

We, _____, the witnesses, sign our names to this instrument, being first duly sworn, and do hereby declare to the undersigned authority that the testator signs and executes this instrument as the testator's will and that the testator

1) signs it willingly
or
2) IF RELEVANT TO YOUR SITUATION: willingly directs another to sign for the testator

and that each of us, in the presence and hearing of the testator, hereby signs this will as witness to the testator's signing, and that to the best of our knowledge the testator is 18 years of age or older, of sound mind, and under no constraint or undue influence.

_____
Witness

_____
Witness

State of _____
County of _____

Subscribed, sworn to, and acknowledged before me by _____, the testator, and subscribed and sworn to before me by _____, and _____ Witnesses, this _____ day of _____, _____.
(Notary Seal)
(Signed) _____
  Minnesota Notary, Commission Expires: _____
  (Official capacity of Officer)

Page ___ of ___

Last Will and Testament

I, _____ a resident of _____ County, Minnesota do hereby make, publish, and declare this to be my Last Will and Testament, hereby revoking any and all Wills and Codicils heretofore made by me.

FIRST: I direct that all my valid debts and funeral expenses be paid out of my estate as soon after my death as is practicable.

SECOND: I make the following special gifts:

If I have made one of more written lists which have been signed by me, and dated, and otherwise prepared in accordance with the Minnesota law M.S.A. Section 524.2-513, then I give the property described in such list or lists to the person or persons named in such list(s) who survive me. I give all tangible personal property not effectively distributed by the provisions of any such written list to: _____

THIRD: I give, devise, and bequeath all my estate, real, personal, and mixed, of whatever kind and wherever situated, of which I may die seized or possessed, or in which I may have any interest or over which I may have any power of appointment or testamentary disposition, to my children _____

_____

_____,

in equal shares, or their lineal descendants per stirpes.

FOURTH: In the event that any beneficiary fails to survive me by thirty days, then this will shall take effect as if that person had predeceased me.

FIFTH: I hereby nominate, constitute, and appoint _____ as Personal Representative of this, my Last Will and Testament. In the event that such named person is unable or unwilling to serve at any time or for any reason, then I nominate, constitute, and appoint _____ as Personal Representative in the place and stead of the person first named herein. It is my will and I direct that my Personal Representative shall not be required to furnish a bond for the faithful performance of his or her duties in any jurisdiction, any provision of law to the contrary notwithstanding, and I give my Personal Representative full power to administer my estate, including the power to settle claims, pay debts, and sell, lease or exchange real and personal property without court order.

I, _____ the testator, sign my name to this instrument this _____ day of _____, and being first duly sworn, do hereby declare to the undersigned authority that I sign and execute this instrument as my will and that

1) I sign it willingly
   or

Page ___ of ___

2) IF RELEVANT TO YOUR SITUATION: I willingly direct another to sign for me,

and that I execute it as my free and voluntary act for the purposes therein expressed, and that I am 18 years of age or older, of sound mind, and under no constraint or undue influence.

_____
Testator

We, _____, the witnesses, sign our names to this instrument, being first duly sworn, and do hereby declare to the undersigned authority that the testator signs and executes this instrument as the testator's will and that the testator

1) signs it willingly
or
2) IF RELEVANT TO YOUR SITUATION: willingly directs another to sign for the testator

and that each of us, in the presence and hearing of the testator, hereby signs this will as witness to the testator's signing, and that to the best of our knowledge the testator is 18 years of age or older, of sound mind, and under no constraint or undue influence.

_____
Witness

_____
Witness

State of _____
County of _____

Subscribed, sworn to, and acknowledged before me by _____, the testator, and subscribed and sworn to before me by _____, and _____ Witnesses, this _____ day of _____, _____.
(Notary Seal)
(Signed) _____
   Minnesota Notary, Commission Expires: _____
   (Official capacity of Officer)

Last Will and Testament

I, _____ a resident of _____ County, Minnesota do hereby make, publish, and declare this to be my Last Will and Testament, hereby revoking any and all Wills and Codicils heretofore made by me.

FIRST: I direct that all my valid debts and funeral expenses be paid out of my estate as soon after my death as is practicable.

SECOND: I make the following special gifts:

If I have made one of more written lists which have been signed by me, and dated, and otherwise prepared in accordance with the Minnesota law M.S.A. Section 524.2-513, then I give the property described in such list or lists to the person or persons named in such list(s) who survive me. I give all tangible personal property not effectively distributed by the provisions of any such written list to: _____

THIRD: I give, devise, and bequeath all my estate, real, personal, and mixed, of whatever kind and wherever situated, of which I may die seized or possessed, or in which I may have any interest or over which I may have any power of appointment or testamentary disposition, to my children _____

_____

_____,

in equal shares, or their lineal descendants per capita.

FOURTH: In the event that any beneficiary fails to survive me by thirty days, then this will shall take effect as if that person had predeceased me.

FIFTH: I hereby nominate, constitute, and appoint _____ as Personal Representative of this, my Last Will and Testament. In the event that such named person is unable or unwilling to serve at any time or for any reason, then I nominate, constitute, and appoint _____ as Personal Representative in the place and stead of the person first named herein. It is my will and I direct that my Personal Representative shall not be required to furnish a bond for the faithful performance of his or her duties in any jurisdiction, any provision of law to the contrary notwithstanding, and I give my Personal Representative full power to administer my estate, including the power to settle claims, pay debts, and sell, lease or exchange real and personal property without court order.

I, _____ the testator, sign my name to this instrument this _____ day of _____, and being first duly sworn, do hereby declare to the undersigned authority that I sign and execute this instrument as my will and that

1) I sign it willingly
    or

2) IF RELEVANT TO YOUR SITUATION: I willingly direct another to sign for me,

and that I execute it as my free and voluntary act for the purposes therein expressed, and that I am 18 years of age or older, of sound mind, and under no constraint or undue influence.

_____
Testator

We, _____, the witnesses, sign our names to this instrument, being first duly sworn, and do hereby declare to the undersigned authority that the testator signs and executes this instrument as the testator's will and that the testator

1) signs it willingly
or
2) IF RELEVANT TO YOUR SITUATION: willingly directs another to sign for the testator

and that each of us, in the presence and hearing of the testator, hereby signs this will as witness to the testator's signing, and that to the best of our knowledge the testator is 18 years of age or older, of sound mind, and under no constraint or undue influence.

_____
Witness

_____
Witness

State of _____
County of _____

Subscribed, sworn to, and acknowledged before me by _____, the testator, and subscribed and sworn to before me by _____, and _____ Witnesses, this _____ day of _____, _____.
(Notary Seal)
(Signed) _____
    Minnesota Notary, Commission Expires: _____
    (Official capacity of Officer)

Last Will and Testament

I, _____ a resident of _____ County, Minnesota do hereby make, publish, and declare this to be my Last Will and Testament, hereby revoking any and all Wills and Codicils heretofore made by me.

FIRST: I direct that all my valid debts and funeral expenses be paid out of my estate as soon after my death as is practicable.

SECOND: I make the following special gifts:

If I have made one of more written lists which have been signed by me, and dated, and otherwise prepared in accordance with the Minnesota law M.S.A. Section 524.2-513, then I give the property described in such list or lists to the person or persons named in such list(s) who survive me. I give all tangible personal property not effectively distributed by the provisions of any such written list to: _____

THIRD: I give, devise, and bequeath all my estate, real, personal, and mixed, of whatever kind and wherever situated, of which I may die seized or possessed, or in which I may have any interest or over which I may have any power of appointment or testamentary disposition, to the following: _____

_____

_____,

or to the survivor of them.

FOURTH: In the event that any beneficiary fails to survive me by thirty days, then this will shall take effect as if that person had predeceased me.

FIFTH: I hereby nominate, constitute, and appoint _____ as Personal Representative of this, my Last Will and Testament. In the event that such named person is unable or unwilling to serve at any time or for any reason, then I nominate, constitute, and appoint _____ as Personal Representative in the place and stead of the person first named herein. It is my will and I direct that my Personal Representative shall not be required to furnish a bond for the faithful performance of his or her duties in any jurisdiction, any provision of law to the contrary notwithstanding, and I give my Personal Representative full power to administer my estate, including the power to settle claims, pay debts, and sell, lease or exchange real and personal property without court order.

I, _____ the testator, sign my name to this instrument this _____ day of _____, and being first duly sworn, do hereby declare to the undersigned authority that I sign and execute this instrument as my will and that

1) I sign it willingly
   or

Page ___ of ___

2) IF RELEVANT TO YOUR SITUATION: I willingly direct another to sign for me,

and that I execute it as my free and voluntary act for the purposes therein expressed, and that I am 18 years of age or older, of sound mind, and under no constraint or undue influence.

_____
Testator

We, _____, the witnesses, sign our names to this instrument, being first duly sworn, and do hereby declare to the undersigned authority that the testator signs and executes this instrument as the testator's will and that the testator

1) signs it willingly
or
2) IF RELEVANT TO YOUR SITUATION: willingly directs another to sign for the testator

and that each of us, in the presence and hearing of the testator, hereby signs this will as witness to the testator's signing, and that to the best of our knowledge the testator is 18 years of age or older, of sound mind, and under no constraint or undue influence.

_____
Witness

_____
Witness

State of _____
County of _____

Subscribed, sworn to, and acknowledged before me by _____, the testator, and subscribed and sworn to before me by _____, and _____ Witnesses, this _____ day of _____, _____.
(Notary Seal)
(Signed) _____
    Minnesota Notary, Commission Expires: _____
    (Official capacity of Officer)

Page ___ of ___

Last Will and Testament

I, _____ a resident of _____ County, Minnesota do hereby make, publish, and declare this to be my Last Will and Testament, hereby revoking any and all Wills and Codicils heretofore made by me.

FIRST: I direct that all my valid debts and funeral expenses be paid out of my estate as soon after my death as is practicable.

SECOND: I make the following special gifts:

If I have made one of more written lists which have been signed by me, and dated, and otherwise prepared in accordance with the Minnesota law M.S.A. Section 524.2-513, then I give the property described in such list or lists to the person or persons named in such list(s) who survive me. I give all tangible personal property not effectively distributed by the provisions of any such written list to: _____

THIRD: I give, devise, and bequeath all my estate, real, personal, and mixed, of whatever kind and wherever situated, of which I may die seized or possessed, or in which I may have any interest or over which I may have any power of appointment or testamentary disposition, to the following _____
_____
_____,
in equal shares, or their lineal descendants per stirpes.

FOURTH: In the event that any beneficiary fails to survive me by thirty days, then this will shall take effect as if that person had predeceased me.

FIFTH: I hereby nominate, constitute, and appoint _____ as Personal Representative of this, my Last Will and Testament. In the event that such named person is unable or unwilling to serve at any time or for any reason, then I nominate, constitute, and appoint _____ as Personal Representative in the place and stead of the person first named herein. It is my will and I direct that my Personal Representative shall not be required to furnish a bond for the faithful performance of his or her duties in any jurisdiction, any provision of law to the contrary notwithstanding, and I give my Personal Representative full power to administer my estate, including the power to settle claims, pay debts, and sell, lease or exchange real and personal property without court order.

I, _____ the testator, sign my name to this instrument this _____ day of _____, and being first duly sworn, do hereby declare to the undersigned authority that I sign and execute this instrument as my will and that

1) I sign it willingly
   or

Page ___ of ___

105

2) IF RELEVANT TO YOUR SITUATION: I willingly direct another to sign for me,

and that I execute it as my free and voluntary act for the purposes therein expressed, and that I am 18 years of age or older, of sound mind, and under no constraint or undue influence.

_____
Testator

We, _____, the witnesses, sign our names to this instrument, being first duly sworn, and do hereby declare to the undersigned authority that the testator signs and exe-cutes this instrument as the testator's will and that the testator

1) signs it willingly
or
2) IF RELEVANT TO YOUR SITUATION: willingly directs another to sign for the testator

and that each of us, in the presence and hearing of the testator, hereby signs this will as witness to the testator's signing, and that to the best of our knowledge the testator is 18 years of age or older, of sound mind, and under no constraint or undue influence.

_____
Witness

_____
Witness

State of _____
County of _____

Subscribed, sworn to, and acknowledged before me by _____, the testator, and subscribed and sworn to before me by _____, and _____ Witnesses, this _____ day of _____, _____.
(Notary Seal)
(Signed) _____
   Minnesota Notary, Commission Expires: _____
   (Official capacity of Officer)

Self-Proved Will Affidavit
(attach to Will)

STATE OF _____

COUNTY OF _____

We, _____ and _____ testator and the witnesses, respectively, whose names are signed to the attached or foregoing instrument, being first duly sworn, do hereby declare to the undersigned authority that the testator signed and executed the instrument as the testator's will and that the testator had signed willingly (or willingly directed another to sign for the testator), and that the testator executed it as the testator's free and voluntary act for the purposes therein expressed, and each of the witnesses, in the presence and hearing of the testator, signed the will as witness and that to the best of the witness' knowledge the testator was at the time 18 years of age or older, of sound mind, and under no constraint or undue influence.

_____
Testator

_____
Witness

_____
Witness

Subscribed, sworn to, and acknowledged before me by _____, the testator, and subscribed and sworn to before me by _____, and _____ Witnesses, this _____ day of _____, _____

(Notary Seal)

(Signed) _____
(Official capacity of Officer)

Page ___ of ___

_____
Witness

_____
Witness

Subscribed, sworn to, and acknowledged before me by _____, the testator, and subscribed and sworn to before me by _____, and _____ Witnesses, this _____ day of _____, _____.
(Notary Seal)
(Signed) _____
   Minnesota Notary, Commission Expires: _____
   (Official capacity of Officer)

Page ___ of ___

Codicil to the Will of

_____

I, _____, a resident of _____ County, Minnesota declare this to be the first codicil to my Last Will and Testament dated _____ _____, _____.

FIRST: I hereby revoke the clause of my Will which reads as follows:

_____

_____

_____

_____.

SECOND: I hereby add the following clause to my Will: _____

_____

_____

_____.

THIRD: In all other respects I hereby confirm and republish my Last Will and Testament dated _____, _____.

IN WITNESS WHEREOF, I have signed, published, and declared the foregoing instrument as and for a codicil to my Last Will and Testament, this _____ day of _____ _____, _____.

_____

The foregoing instrument was on the _____day of _____, _____, signed at the end thereof, and at the same time published and declared by _____, as and for a codicil to his/her Last Will and Testament, dated _____ _____, _____, in the presence of each of us, who, this attestation clause having been read to us, did at the request of the said testator/testatrix, in his/her presence and in the presence of each other signed our names as witnesses thereto.

_____residing at_____

_____residing at_____

This page intentionally left blank.

Self-Proved Codicil Affidavit
(attach to Will)

STATE OF _____

COUNTY OF _____

We, _____ and _____ testator and the witnesses, respectively, whose names are signed to the attached or foregoing instrument, being first duly sworn, do hereby declare to the undersigned authority that the testator signed and executed the attached or foregoing instrument as a codicil to the testator's will; and that the testator had signed willingly (or willingly directed another to sign for the testator), and that the testator executed it as the testator's free and voluntary act for the purposes therein expressed, and each of the witnesses, in the presence and hearing of the testator, signed the will as witness and that to the best of the witness' knowledge the testator was at the time 18 years of age or older, of sound mind, and under no constraint or undue influence.

_____
Testator

_____
Witness

_____
Witness

Subscribed, sworn to, and acknowledged before me by _____, the testator, and subscribed and sworn to before me by _____, and _____ Witnesses, this _____ day of _____, _____

(Notary Seal)

(Signed) _____
   Minnesota Notary, Commission Expires: _____
   (Official capacity of Officer)

This page intentionally left blank.

Health Care Directive

I, _____, born on_____ am an
adult of sound mind. I willfully and voluntarily make this statement as a directive to be followed
if I have a terminal illness or injury and if I become unable to participate in decisions regarding
my health care. I understand that my health care providers are legally bound to act consistently
with my wishes, within the limits of reasonable medical practice and other applicable law.

I also recognize that it is my right to make medical and health care decisions for myself as long as
I am able to do so. I understand too that I may revoke this directive at any time.

The following are my feelings and wishes regarding my health care.
First, this is my philosophy, my spiritual beliefs and traditions:

Second, my health care goals are:

Third, these are my anxieties and fears about health care:

Fourth, I believe life is no longer worth living if:

Fifth, this is how I think my beliefs about my medical condition could affect my family:

These are my **instructions** for my health care. I know what I do and do not want.

I want to be able to have many medical treatments to improve my medical condition, to save or prolong my life. My health care providers may use artificial breathing machines connected to a tube in my lungs, artificial fluids or feeding through tubes. If my heart stops, they may try to restart it. They may perform surgeries, kidney dialysis and give me medications, antibiotics and blood transfusions. These types of treatments and most other medical treatment may be tried until they no longer help me.

If I were temporarily unable to decide for myself or speak or communicate for myself, I would want:

If I were dying and unable to decide for myself or speak or communicate for myself, I would want:

If I were in a coma or unconscious and would never wake up, I would want:

If I become completely dependent on other people for my care and no longer able to decide for myself or speak or communicate on my own, I would want:

No matter what is happening to me, my doctors will try to reduce my pain and keep me comfortable. If pain relief affects my alertness or may shorten my life, this is how I feel and what I believe:

114

There are other things that I want for my health care:

There are things that I do **not** want for my health care:

This is where I want to receive my health care:

I have certain feelings about my dying process:

I want to die at this type of location or at this specific place:

I have other wishes about my dying process:

I do or do **not** (circle either do or do **not**) want to donate some or all (circle either some or all) of my body. If some: list which parts and your feelings about this gift:

This is how I want by remains to be handled: (cremation, burial):

Use the space below to communicate any other thoughts or wishes you have about your health care:

MY HEALTH CARE AGENT

I know that a health care agent is not required. But I have decided to appoint an agent to make my health care decisions for me **if** I am no longer able to decide for myself or speak or communicate on my own. I understand that it is my right to change my agent whenever I want to.

WHEN I am no longer able to decide for myself or speak or communicate on my own I trust and **appoint**_____
as my health care **agent** to make health care decisions for me.

Relationship of my health care agent to me:_____

Telephone number of my health care agent: (____) _____

Address of my health care agent:_____

_____

If my health care agent is not reasonably available, I trust and **appoint** _____

_____

as my **alternate** or backup health care **agent** to make health care decisions for me when I am no longer able to decide for myself or speak or communicate on my own.

Relationship of my alternate health care agent to me:_____

Telephone number of my alternate health care agent: (____)_____

Address of my alternate health care agent:_____

116

If I am no longer able to decide for myself or speak or communicate on my own, I give my agent the following powers:

1. My health care agent must follow my health care instructions in this document and any other instructions that I have given to this agent.

2. If I have not given my health care agent any instructions, then this person must act in my best interests.

3. If I am no longer able to decide for myself or speak or communicate on my own, my health care agent has the power to:

    *   Make any and all of my health care decisions for me. This power includes the right to give, refuse or take back consent to any care, treatment, services or procedures. It also includes the power to decide to start or stop treatment that is keeping me alive or might keep me alive. And, it includes the power to decide about intrusive mental health treatment.

    *   Decide who my health care providers should be.

    *   Choose where I live and where I receive care and support relative to my health care needs.

    *   Have the same rights as I have to review my medical records and to give them to others.

4. There are some powers I do not want my health care agent to have. These are:

5. My health care agent has the following powers **ONLY if** I have initialed them:

    _____to decide if my organs should be donated when I die.
    (Your initials)

    _____to decide if I will be buried or cremated when I die.
    (Your initials)

I have made this health care directive a legal document by signing it and I have it made official by having a notary public sign it

<u>or</u>

I have had two witnesses sign it.

I am thinking clearly. I agree with everything that is in my health care directive. And, I have willingly made this directive.

_____

(My signature)

_____

(Date Signed)

_____

(My date of birth)

_____

(My address)

If I cannot sign my name, I can ask someone to sign this health care directive for me.

_____

(Signature of Person who I asked to sign this health care directive for me)

_____

(Printed name of person who I asked to sign this health care directive for me)

If two witnesses sign, fill in the following:

NOTE: ONLY <u>ONE</u> OF THESE WITNESSES CAN BE MY HEALTH CARE PROVIDER OR EMPLOYEE OF ONE OF MY HEALTH CARE PROVIDERS ON THE DAY I SIGN THIS DIRECTIVE.

Witness number 1

On _____ in my presence, _____

 (Date)   (Name)

acknowledged her/his signature on this health care directive

or

acknowledged that she/he authorized the person signing this health care directive to sign on her/his behalf.

118

I am at least 18 years of age.

I am not named as a health care agent or alternate health care agent in this document.

NOTE: IF APPROPRIATE: I am a health care provider or an employee of a health care provider giving direct care to the person making this health care directive, I have put my initials in this space:_____.

I certify that the information in my above oath is true and correct.

_____

(Signature of Witness number 1)

Witness number 2

On _____in my presence, _____

 (Date)   (Name)

acknowledged her/his signature on this health care directive

or

acknowledged that she/he authorized the person signing this health care directive to sign on her/his behalf.

I am at least 18 years of age.

I am not named as a health care agent or alternate health care agent in this document.

NOTE: IF APPROPRIATE: I am a health care provider or an employee of a health care provider giving direct care to the person making this health care directive, I have put my initials in this space:_____.

I certify that the information in my above oath is true and correct.

_____

(Signature of Witness number 2)

**USE AS MANY ADDITIONAL PAGES AS YOU NEED
TO COMMUNICATE YOUR INSTRUCTIONS.
ATTACH EACH ADDITIONAL PAGE TO THIS DOCUMENT.**

ANATOMICAL DONOR CARD

The undersigned hereby makes this anatomical gift, if medically acceptable, to take effect on death. The words and marks below indicate my desires:

I give:

        (a) _____ any needed organs or parts;

        (b) _____ only the following organs or parts

_____

for the purpose of transplantation, therapy, medical research, or education;

        (c) _____ my body for anatomical study if needed.

Limitations or special wishes, if any:

_____

_____   _____
Signature of Donor   Date of Birth

_____   _____
Date Signed   City & State

ANATOMICAL DONOR CARD

The undersigned hereby makes this anatomical gift, if medically acceptable, to take effect on death. The words and marks below indicate my desires:

I give:

        (a) _____ any needed organs or parts;

        (b) _____ only the following organs or parts

_____

for the purpose of transplantation, therapy, medical research, or education;

        (c) _____ my body for anatomical study if needed.

Limitations or special wishes, if any:

_____

_____   _____
Signature of Donor   Date of Birth

_____   _____
Date Signed   City & State

ANATOMICAL DONOR CARD

The undersigned hereby makes this anatomical gift, if medically acceptable, to take effect on death. The words and marks below indicate my desires:

I give:

        (a) _____ any needed organs or parts;

        (b) _____ only the following organs or parts

_____

for the purpose of transplantation, therapy, medical research, or education;

        (c) _____ my body for anatomical study if needed.

Limitations or special wishes, if any:

_____

_____   _____
Signature of Donor   Date of Birth

_____   _____
Date Signed   City & State

ANATOMICAL DONOR CARD

The undersigned hereby makes this anatomical gift, if medically acceptable, to take effect on death. The words and marks below indicate my desires:

I give:

        (a) _____ any needed organs or parts;

        (b) _____ only the following organs or parts

_____

for the purpose of transplantation, therapy, medical research, or education;

        (c) _____ my body for anatomical study if needed.

Limitations or special wishes, if any:

_____

_____   _____
Signature of Donor   Date of Birth

_____   _____
Date Signed   City & State

One of these cards should be cut out and carried in your wallet or purse.

INDEX

T

W

SPHINX® PUBLISHING'S NATIONAL TITLES
Valid in All 50 States

LEGAL SURVIVAL IN BUSINESS

The Complete Book of Corporate Forms	$24.95
How to Form a Delaware Corporation from Any State	$24.95
How to Form a Limited Liability Company	$22.95
Incorporate in Nevada from Any State	$24.95
How to Form a Nonprofit Corporation	$24.95
How to Form Your Own Corporation (3E)	$24.95
How to Form Your Own Partnership	$22.95
How to Register Your Own Copyright (3E)	$21.95
How to Register Your Own Trademark (3E)	$21.95
Most Valuable Business Legal Forms You'll Ever Need (3E)	$21.95

LEGAL SURVIVAL IN COURT

Crime Victim's Guide to Justice (2E)	$21.95
Grandparents' Rights (3E)	$24.95
Help Your Lawyer Win Your Case (2E)	$14.95
Jurors' Rights (2E)	$12.95
Legal Research Made Easy (2E)	$16.95
Winning Your Personal Injury Claim (2E)	$24.95
Your Rights When You Owe Too Much	$16.95

LEGAL SURVIVAL IN REAL ESTATE

Essential Guide to Real Estate Contracts	$18.95
Essential Guide to Real Estate Leases	$18.95
How to Buy a Condominium or Townhome	$19.95

LEGAL SURVIVAL IN PERSONAL AFFAIRS

Cómo Hacer su Propio Testamento	$16.95
Guía de Inmigración a Estados Unidos (2E)	$24.95
Cómo Solicitar su Propio Divorcio	$24.95
How to File Your Own Bankruptcy (4E)	$21.95
How to File Your Own Divorce (4E)	$24.95
How to Make Your Own Will (2E)	$16.95
How to Write Your Own Living Will (2E)	$16.95
How to Write Your Own Premarital Agreement (2E)	$21.95
How to Win Your Unemployment Compensation Claim	$21.95
Living Trusts and Simple Ways to Avoid Probate (2E)	$22.95
Most Valuable Personal Legal Forms You'll Ever Need	$24.95
Neighbor v. Neighbor (2E)	$16.95
The Nanny and Domestic Help Legal Kit	$22.95
The Power of Attorney Handbook (3E)	$19.95
Repair Your Own Credit and Deal with Debt	$18.95
The Social Security Benefits Handbook (3E)	$18.95
Unmarried Parents' Rights	$19.95
U.S.A. Immigration Guide (3E)	$19.95
Your Right to Child Custody, Visitation and Support (2E)	$24.95

Legal Survival Guides are directly available from Sourcebooks, Inc., or from your local bookstores.
Prices are subject to change without notice.

For credit card orders call 1–800–432–7444, write P.O. Box 4410, Naperville, IL 60567-4410
or fax 630-961-2168

SPHINX® PUBLISHING ORDER FORM

BILL TO:		SHIP TO:	
Phone #	Terms	F.O.B. Chicago, IL	Ship Date

Charge my: VISA   MasterCard   American Express

Money Order or Personal Check

Credit Card Number   Expiration Date

Qty	ISBN	Title	Retail	Ext.
		SPHINX PUBLISHING NATIONAL TITLES		
	1-57248-148-X	Cómo Hacer su Propio Testamento	$16.95	
	1-57248-147-1	Cómo Solicitar su Propio Divorcio	$24.95	
	1-57248-166-8	The Complete Book of Corporate Forms	$24.95	
	1-57248-163-3	Crime Victim's Guide to Justice (2E)	$21.95	
	1-57248-159-5	Essential Guide to Real Estate Contracts	$18.95	
	1-57248-160-9	Essential Guide to Real Estate Leases	$18.95	
	1-57248-139-0	Grandparents' Rights (3E)	$24.95	
	1-57248-087-4	Guía de Inmigración a Estados Unidos (2E)	$24.95	
	1-57248-103-X	Help Your Lawyer Win Your Case (2E)	$14.95	
	1-57071-164-X	How to Buy a Condominium or Townhome	$19.95	
	1-57071-223-9	How to File Your Own Bankruptcy (4E)	$21.95	
	1-57248-132-3	How to File Your Own Divorce (4E)	$24.95	
	1-57248-100-5	How to Form a DE Corporation from Any State	$24.95	
	1-57248-083-1	How to Form a Limited Liability Company	$22.95	
	1-57248-099-8	How to Form a Nonprofit Corporation	$24.95	
	1-57248-133-1	How to Form Your Own Corporation (3E)	$24.95	
	1-57071-343-X	How to Form Your Own Partnership	$22.95	
	1-57248-119-6	How to Make Your Own Will (2E)	$16.95	
	1-57248-124-2	How to Register Your Own Copyright (3E)	$21.95	
	1-57248-104-8	How to Register Your Own Trademark (3E)	$21.95	
	1-57071-349-9	How to Win Your Unemployment Compensation Claim	$21.95	
	1-57248-118-8	How to Write Your Own Living Will (2E)	$16.95	
	1-57071-344-8	How to Write Your Own Premarital Agreement (2E)	$21.95	
	1-57248-158-7	Incorporate in Nevada from Any State	$24.95	
	1-57071-333-2	Jurors' Rights (2E)	$12.95	
	1-57071-400-2	Legal Research Made Easy (2E)	$16.95	
	1-57071-336-7	Living Trusts and Simple Ways to Avoid Probate (2E)	$22.95	

Qty	ISBN	Title	Retail	Ext.
	1-57248-167-6	Most Valuable Bus. Legal Forms You'll Ever Need (3E)	$21.95	
	1-57248-130-7	Most Valuable Personal Legal Forms You'll Ever Need	$24.95	
	1-57248-098-X	The Nanny and Domestic Help Legal Kit	$22.95	
	1-57248-089-0	Neighbor v. Neighbor (2E)	$16.95	
	1-57071-348-0	The Power of Attorney Handbook (3E)	$19.95	
	1-57248-149-8	Repair Your Own Credit and Deal with Debt	$18.95	
	1-57248-168-4	The Social Security Benefits Handbook (3E)	$18.95	
	1-57071-399-5	Unmarried Parents' Rights	$19.95	
	1-57071-354-5	U.S.A. Immigration Guide (3E)	$19.95	
	1-57248-138-2	Winning Your Personal Injury Claim (2E)	$24.95	
	1-57248-162-5	Your Right to Child Custody, Visitation and Support (2E)	$24.95	
	1-57248-157-9	Your Rights When You Owe Too Much	$16.95	
		CALIFORNIA TITLES		
	1-57248-150-1	CA Power of Attorney Handbook (2E)	$18.95	
	1-57248-151-X	How to File for Divorce in CA (3E)	$26.95	
	1-57071-356-1	How to Make a CA Will	$16.95	
	1-57248-145-5	How to Probate and Settle an Estate in California	$26.95	
	1-57248-146-3	How to Start a Business in CA	$18.95	
	1-57071-358-8	How to Win in Small Claims Court in CA	$16.95	
	1-57071-359-6	Landlords' Rights and Duties in CA	$21.95	
		FLORIDA TITLES		
	1-57071-363-4	Florida Power of Attorney Handbook (2E)	$16.95	
	1-57248-176-5	How to File for Divorce in FL (7E)	$26.95	
	1-57248-177-3	How to Form a Corporation in FL (5E)	$24.95	
	1-57248-086-6	How to Form a Limited Liability Co. in FL	$22.95	
	1-57071-401-0	How to Form a Partnership in FL	$22.95	
	1-57248-113-7	How to Make a FL Will (6E)	$16.95	
	Form Continued on Following Page		**SUBTOTAL**	

To order, call Sourcebooks at 1-800-432-7444 or FAX (630) 961-2168 (Bookstores, libraries, wholesalers—please call for discount)

Prices are subject to change without notice.

SPHINX® PUBLISHING ORDER FORM

Qty	ISBN	Title	Retail	Ext.
	1-57248-088-2	How to Modify Your FL Divorce Judgment (4E)	$24.95	
	1-57248-144-7	How to Probate and Settle an Estate in FL (4E)	$26.95	
	1-57248-081-5	How to Start a Business in FL (5E)	$16.95	
	1-57071-362-6	How to Win in Small Claims Court in FL (6E)	$16.95	
	1-57248-123-4	Landlords' Rights and Duties in FL (8E)	$21.95	
	GEORGIA TITLES			
	1-57248-137-4	How to File for Divorce in GA (4E)	$21.95	
	1-57248-075-0	How to Make a GA Will (3E)	$16.95	
	1-57248-140-4	How to Start a Business in Georgia (2E)	$16.95	
	ILLINOIS TITLES			
	1-57071-405-3	How to File for Divorce in IL (2E)	$21.95	
	1-57071-415-0	How to Make an IL Will (2E)	$16.95	
	1-57071-416-9	How to Start a Business in IL (2E)	$18.95	
	1-57248-078-5	Landlords' Rights & Duties in IL	$21.95	
	MASSACHUSETTS TITLES			
	1-57248-128-5	How to File for Divorce in MA (3E)	$24.95	
	1-57248-115-3	How to Form a Corporation in MA	$24.95	
	1-57248-108-0	How to Make a MA Will (2E)	$16.95	
	1-57248-106-4	How to Start a Business in MA (2E)	$18.95	
	1-57248-107-2	Landlords' Rights and Duties in MA (2E)	$21.95	
	MICHIGAN TITLES			
	1-57071-409-6	How to File for Divorce in MI (2E)	$21.95	
	1-57248-077-7	How to Make a MI Will (2E)	$16.95	
	1-57071-407-X	How to Start a Business in MI (2E)	$16.95	
	MINNESOTA TITLES			
	1-57248-142-0	How to File for Divorce in MN	$21.95	
	1-57248-178-1	How to Make a MN Will (2E)	$16.95	
	NEW YORK TITLES			
	1-57248-141-2	How to File for Divorce in NY (2E)	$26.95	
	1-57248-105-6	How to Form a Corporation in NY	$24.95	
	1-57248-095-5	How to Make a NY Will (2E)	$16.95	
	1-57071-185-2	How to Start a Business in NY	$18.95	
	1-57071-187-9	How to Win in Small Claims Court in NY	$16.95	

Qty	ISBN	Title	Retail	Ext.
	1-57071-186-0	Landlords' Rights and Duties in NY	$21.95	
	1-57071-188-7	New York Power of Attorney Handbook	$19.95	
	1-57248-122-6	Tenants' Rights in NY	$21.95	
	NORTH CAROLINA TITLES			
	1-57248-185-4	How to File for Divorce in NC (3E)	$22.95	
	1-57248-129-3	How to Make a NC Will (3E)	$16.95	
	1-57248-184-6	How to Start a Business in NC (3E)	$18.95	
	1-57248-091-2	Landlords' Rights & Duties in NC	$21.95	
	OHIO TITLES			
	1-57248-190-0	How to File for Divorce in OH (2E)	$24.95	
	1-57248-174-9	How to Form a Corporation in Ohio	$24.95	
	PENNSYLVANIA TITLES			
	1-57248-127-7	How to File for Divorce in PA (2E)	$24.95	
	1-57248-094-7	How to Make a PA Will (2E)	$16.95	
	1-57248-112-9	How to Start a Business in PA (2E)	$18.95	
	1-57071-179-8	Landlords' Rights and Duties in PA	$19.95	
	TEXAS TITLES			
	1-57248-171-4	Child Custody, Visitation, and Support in TX	$22.95	
	1-57071-330-8	How to File for Divorce in TX (2E)	$21.95	
	1-57248-114-5	How to Form a Corporation in TX (2E)	$24.95	
	1-57071-417-7	How to Make a TX Will (2E)	$16.95	
	1-57071-418-5	How to Probate an Estate in TX (2E)	$22.95	
	1-57071-365-0	How to Start a Business in TX (2E)	$18.95	
	1-57248-111-0	How to Win in Small Claims Court in TX (2E)	$16.95	
	1-57248-110-2	Landlords' Rights and Duties in TX (2E)	$21.95	

SUBTOTAL THIS PAGE _____

SUBTOTAL PREVIOUS PAGE _____

Shipping — $5.00 for 1st book, $1.00 each additional _____

Illinois residents add 6.75% sales tax _____

Connecticut residents add 6.00% sales tax _____

TOTAL _____

To order, call Sourcebooks at 1-800-432-7444 or FAX (630) 961-2168 (Bookstores, libraries, wholesalers—please call for discount)
Prices are subject to change without notice.